THE GOSPEL OF MARK

GW00634706

By the same author

LANDMARKS IN THE STORY OF CHRISTIANITY

THE LIFE OF CHRIST

THE STUDY OF THE GOSPELS

THE ACTS OF THE APOSTLES

A CRITICAL INTRODUCTION TO THE GOSPELS

THE SYNOPTIC GOSPELS

WHO'S WHO IN THE GOSPELS

THE CHURCH IN THE NEW TESTAMENT

THE GOSPEL OF MATTHEW

THE GOSPEL OF LUKE

THE FOURTH GOSPEL

The Gospel of
Mark

H. A. GUY, B.D., B.A.

Macmillan Education

First Edition 1968
Reprinted 1969, 1971, 1973, 1974, 1976 (twice), 1978

Published by
MACMILLAN EDUCATION LIMITED
Houndmills Basingstoke Hampshire RG21 2XS and London
Associated companies in Delhi Dublin
Hong Kong Johannesburg Lagos Melbourne
New York Singapore and Tokyo

ISBN 0 333 03924 6

Printed in Hong Kong by
Wing King Tong Co Ltd

CONTENTS

PREFACE   vii

INTRODUCTION   1

The approach to the Gospels—Different kinds of criticism—The Synoptic Gospels—The priority of Mark—
The nature of the book—The oral period—The writing
of the Gospel—The materials used by Mark—The
characteristics of the book—The author of the Gospel
—The date of the Gospel—The structure of Mark's
Gospel—Different views of the book

MAP OF PALESTINE   44

SUMMARY OF CONTENTS OF
    THE GOSPEL   45

Chapter   I. The first activities of Jesus   49

Chapter   II. Opposition to Jesus   61

Chapter   III. Further causes of opposi-
                tion and misunderstanding   70

Chapter   IV. Teaching by parables   77

Chapter   V. Jesus' works of power   86

Chapter   VI. Further Galilean activities   91

Chapter VII. Further opposition and journeys outside Galilee 101

Chapter VIII. On the way to Caesarea Philippi 108

Chapter IX. Return from the north to Capernaum 119

Chapter X. The journey towards Jerusalem 128

Chapter XI. Jesus in Jerusalem 137

Chapter XII. Controversy in Jerusalem 144

Chapter XIII. Apocalyptic teaching 154

Chapter XIV. The triumph of Jesus' enemies 163

Chapter XV. The trial and execution of Jesus 176

Chapter XVI. After the crucifixion 185

INDEX OF SUBJECTS 190

PREFACE

THE Gospel of Mark might well be called the most important book in the world—for the Christian world, at any rate. It was a pioneer effort, the first attempt at a comprehensive account of the life of Jesus of Nazareth. In its early days, however, it seems to have been but little appreciated. As soon as the other Gospels came into circulation, with their fuller narratives of the ministry of Jesus and their emphasis on his teaching as well as his deeds, Mark dropped into the background. Church leaders and writers quoted from Matthew or Luke in preference to Mark. Since most of the matter in Mark is to be found in the other two Synoptics, there was a danger that the book might be so neglected as to be lost altogether, if it had not been for its traditional association with the apostle Peter.

In our own day, however, this Gospel has at last come into its own. This century has been characterised, in the study of the Gospels, by the attention given to Mark. As soon as it was established, over a century ago now, that Mark was the first of the Gospels to be written and had been used as a source by the writers of Matthew and Luke, it was realised by scholars that Synoptic study was dependent to a great extent on a thorough understanding of Mark's Gospel.

This is true also for those lesser folk—the ordinary student, the candidate for examinations, the 'general reader'—for whom this book is intended. To know the contents of Mark and to understand its nature is an essential prerequisite for studying the other Gospels. Hence it is hoped that this book will be of use not only to those who wish to make a special study of Mark but to all who are interested in the contents of the Gospels or indeed in the message of the whole New Testament.

Students who use this book would do well to read through Mark's Gospel first of all, in any translation which they find easy or interesting, preferably one with which they are not familiar. This could well be done at a sitting; there are few who would not profit from this. Then a study should be made chapter by chapter, with the notes provided here. Candidates for examinations should make their own summaries of discussions or arguments. It would then be a help to read through the Gospel again, with the further insight gained into the matter and message of the book. For revision for an examination, as well as for general reference, use should be made of the index of subjects.

The text of the Gospel is not printed here, for it is assumed that the reader will have a copy of the Gospel by him. The book may be used with any English translation. References are made to the Revised Version of 1881 (abbreviated as R.V.), the Revised Standard Version of 1946 (R.S.V.) and the New English Bible of 1961 (N.E.B.). One or other of these is generally specified for examination purposes. They are all to be preferred to the Authorised Version of 1611 for correctness of text, accuracy and fidelity to the Greek. Translations by individuals such as R. F. Weymouth, J. Moffatt, E. V. Rieu and R. Knox are often helpful in illuminating passages which may present difficulties in the more conventional renderings.

H. A. G.

Worcester, 1967

INTRODUCTION

In reading any book, much depends on the way in which we approach it. This will affect what we expect to find in it and how far we are satisfied with what we do find there. Our attitude towards a novel is different from the way in which we read a scientific treatise or an historical narrative. We read some books more critically than others and this naturally affects our judgment of their contents. The question how we are to read the Gospels, or indeed any part of the Bible, is one that people seldom consciously ask themselves. How far can we apply to these books the same attitude and standards of judgment that we use in the case of other types of literature—or are we to regard them as completely different from any other books we may read?

For centuries one way of looking at the Gospels was to consider them as true in every word, every statement in them to be accepted without question, simply because, it was held, God had instructed the writers what to put down. This is the theory of 'verbal inspiration'. It is based on the 'all or none' principle but it is doubtful if people who hold this view carry it out to its logical conclusion. This would be to make the writers of the books mere machines, computers which God had programmed and they automatically produced the answers. God is thought of as dictating what they had to put down, without allowing for their human characteristics and differences. This theory also does not fit the facts. It breaks down as soon as we read the Gospels intelligently and compare one account with another. Why should God inspire one man to say that James and John came to Jesus with a request for the chief places for themselves, but tell another man to write that their mother came? (Mark x. 35; Matt. xx. 20) Why should he instruct Mark to write a full and vivid account of many a healing act of Jesus but inspire Matthew to give a shorter and considerably less vivid narrative? Why, if both writers were inerrant, should Matthew say that a Roman centurion came to Jesus with a request for him to heal his servant, while in Luke's account the centurion never appears at all but sends his message through others? (Matt. viii. 5ff.; Luke vii. 3ff.) Why did God tell Mark that three women, on visiting the tomb of Jesus, saw a young man sitting inside, when he apparently told Matthew that it was an angel who was sitting on a stone outside the tomb, but told Luke that two men were standing there, while John was instructed that one woman saw two angels inside the tomb? If they were both verbally inspired, how is it that the author of Matthew says that the priests bought a 'field of blood' after the death of Judas with the money that he had returned to them, while Luke relates that Judas himself bought it with the money and afterwards fell in it and died? (Matt. xxvii. 7–8; Acts i. 18–19) If God inspired all these writers equally, he was contradicting himself.

If it is replied that God must work through the individual and allow each author to write in his own style and use his intelligence, this surrenders the whole case for 'verbal inspiration'. The theory indeed does not arise from study of the books of the Bible but from a preconceived notion of 'inspiration' which will not bear examination when confronted with the facts. It is not indeed Christian but is more like a Moslem idea of God's activity in relation to men.

If we abandon this view, we must approach the Gospels in a different frame of mind, not accepting without examination the statements made, but using our powers of understanding and judgment. This means that we must study the books 'critically'. This is a term which, when popularly used, often conveys a wrong impression. 'Criticism' is derived from a Greek word, *kritēs*, which means a judge. Criticism means the careful and systematic study of a subject by one who is qualified to exercise his judgment. Criticism of this kind does not mean fault-finding. In many cases it should rather be termed appreciation. When we express an opinion about any work of art or literature, we are acting as a critic.

The reader who is not familiar with this approach to the Gospels would do well to bear these considerations in mind in his study of Mark. He may find in these pages some suggestions which are new to him and which seem at first sight to conflict with ideas or presuppositions with which he has been long familiar. He must not reject them off-hand because of this. He must be prepared to act as a critic—a judge—and decide for himself whether such views are probable in the light of the evidence and whether they have value in helping towards an understanding of the Gospel as a whole or an understanding of the work of Jesus.

DIFFERENT KINDS OF CRITICISM

There are various departments of literary criticism, as it has been described above—scientific study, judgment or appreciation. Textual (or Lower) Criticism is an attempt to discover the original words as written by the author, the study of the 'text' of a book. In the case of books composed and printed in modern times this is comparatively easy. But when we come to consider books which were produced before the invention of printing in Europe (i.e. all writings before the end of the fifteenth century), we have to rely on handwritten copies or manuscripts, made in some cases much later than the original. The first copy of a book written by hand soon perished. In no case have we the original manuscript of any Greek or Latin writer, whether Homer, Julius Caesar, Horace, Tacitus, Mark or Paul. We have to deal with copies made by scribes. It is obviously too much to expect that they would always copy exactly, without making any mistakes or alterations. Hence there arise different 'readings' in the manuscripts. Sometimes these consist only of one word or even a letter, but occasionally texts differ to the extent of a whole sentence or paragraph. There are variants in the texts of all classical authors.

This applies also to the New Testament books. Each book was of course produced quite separately, written on papyrus. The Christian scribe would no doubt exercise great care in copying a Gospel or an Epistle but, not being a professional, he would not be so proficient at his task. His eyes must often have been strained and his hand got tired; however careful and conscientious he might be, it was inevitable that he made some slips. He might omit a word or a phrase or a whole line; he might inadvertently repeat a word or a letter or mistake one Greek letter or abbreviation for another. Occasionally scribes seem to have deliberately altered the text before them, in copying, in order to make a passage run more smoothly or to make a passage agree with a parallel account in another Gospel; occasionally (but not often) they even made additions or alterations to introduce or stress a point of Christian doctrine.

The task of the textual critic is to seek to discover the true text—the words which were actually written by the author. For this purpose he has at his disposal, in the case of the New Testament, a vast amount of material. This consists of manuscripts in Greek (written on papyrus in the case of earlier ones and on vellum later on), of translations into other languages in the early centuries (such as Syriac, Latin, Egyptian, Armenian) and of quotations in early Christian writers (which show the kind of text which was current in their time).

Another department of literary criticism is concerned with the task of discovering the sources from which a writer gained his information. In the case of a modern book this is comparatively easy, for the author would acknowledge his indebtedness to previous writers on his subject by supplying a book list or by footnotes in the text; if he makes a quotation, this is indicated in the print. But no such devices were used in the ancient world, neither was there any question of copyright, so an author would frequently make use of someone else's work and incorporate it in his own, either rewriting a passage in his own words or quoting it verbatim or with some alterations. The source was not generally acknowledged. This was an accepted literary practice and can be exemplified from almost any Greek or Latin writer and from both the Old Testament and the New Testament books.

This Source Criticism is a department of the study known as Higher Criticism—in contrast to the Lower (or Textual) Criticism. These terms are adopted from the metaphor of a river. The higher critic seeks to penetrate higher up the stream, nearer the source (which is the actual writing of the book). He discusses questions of the composition of a book, the methods of the writer, its date and authorship. The textual critic deals with matters lower down the stream, after the book has been written and copies made and circulated.

A third type of study is called Form Criticism—the study of the 'forms' which the material took before it was incorporated into the written book. This is dealt with later on (pp. 14 ff.).

THE SYNOPTIC GOSPELS

It is plain to any discerning reader that a distinction has to be made between the first three Gospels and the fourth. Matthew, Mark and Luke give a similar account of the work of Jesus and see it from much the same point of view. They are hence classed together as the Synoptic Gospels (Greek: *sun*, together, and *opsis*, a view or sight). The term also refers to the fact that many passages in the three books can be arranged in parallel columns and thus 'seen together' in a synopsis. This in itself constitutes a problem: why is it that the three are so much alike? At the same time, why do they differ in many ways?

The facts which constitute the synoptic problem are these: first, all three books have the same general out-line of the life of Jesus. (This is given on pp. 34 ff.) Many narratives are related in all three or in two of them. When one or two of the Gospels diverge from the common order of events, they always return to it. Further, we find in parallel passages, whether of inci-dent or of teaching, a remarkable verbal similarity;

sometimes the wording is almost identical for whole sentences. But there are differences between the three as well as close similarities. There are some variations in the order, within the same general framework. In parallel passages the wording is not exactly the same. Sometimes it seems that one Gospel has the more vivid phrase or the more accurate statement. A further difficulty is that each Gospel has matter which is not found elsewhere. This is very little in the case of Mark but far more extensive in the other two.

. The similarities show that there must be some connection between the three books; the differences show that they must have been written independently.

Various solutions of this problem have been put forward. One was the 'oral hypothesis'—that each writer was dependent simply on oral tradition. Writing independently, the three happened to use similar language and kept to the same order because they adhered faithfully to the oral accounts. But this assumes that the oral tradition had a fixed form not only in wording but in the order of events. This is very unlikely; oral tradition is not carried on like that, but in separate fragments. Incidents and teaching are remembered as independent episodes. Examination of the parallel accounts in the Gospels further shows that the differences are often due to stylistic or grammatical alterations, suggesting the use of written documents. A literary connection is demanded by the facts.

The earliest documentary solution was that Matthew was written first and was abbreviated to produce the shorter Gospel of Mark. But in parallel narratives, Mark's account is almost always the longer one, so the writer was not 'abbreviating' Matthew. It is also a much more vivid and lifelike account than Matthew's, which is often tame in comparison and omits vital details. Another objection to this view is that much valuable matter in Jesus' teaching is not found in Mark —material which no 'abbreviator' would think of omitting.

Another documentary theory was that all three writers used a primitive Gospel which has disappeared. This might account for the places where the three agree; but what of the passages which are common to Matthew and Luke but not found in Mark, or the matter peculiar to one Gospel?

The view which has been generally accepted for several generations now is the two-source theory: that the first Gospel was Mark, which was used by the writers of Matthew and Luke, and that in addition these two employed a collection of Jesus' teaching. This document is called Q (from the German *Quelle*, meaning source) and from it were taken the parallel passages in Matthew and Luke. An extension of this view is the four-document hypothesis put forward by B. H. Streeter: that in addition to using Mark and Q, the writer of Matthew had special traditions, both narrative and teaching (called for convenience M), while Luke used special matter (called L). In each case this material may have been oral or written.

THE PRIORITY OF MARK

There are several arguments which lead to the conclusion that the first of our Gospels was Mark, a view first put forward by C. Lachmann in 1835.

(i) Almost the whole of this Gospel is contained in Matthew or Luke or both. Ninety-five per cent of it is in Matthew, about sixty-five per cent in Luke. There are only about thirty verses in Mark which have no parallel elsewhere.

(ii) The general order of events throughout is Mark's. Sometimes Matthew and sometimes Luke departs from the Markan narrative, but they never do so at the same point and they always return to it. Matthew diverges to insert additional teaching matter or to rearrange incidents, but always comes back to Mark's order. Luke gives blocks of Markan matter alternating with sections of other material; the Markan blocks are in the same order as in that Gospel.

(iii) Comparison of the language in the three books shows a similar situation. More than half the Greek words used in Mark are reproduced in parallel sections in the other two. Where Matthew or Luke diverges, the other one generally remains faithful to Mark's wording. Arrangement of the material and the language thus both suggest that Mark is the common basis.

(iv) Mark is the shortest of the three. It is far more likely that the other writers made use of this brief book and expanded it with other material, rather than that the writer of Mark attempted a 'cut' version of either of the others. Mark consists mainly of narrative, the activities of Jesus. The other writers used this basic portrait of Jesus and his work, each one adding to it in his own way—Matthew to emphasise the appeal of Jesus to the Jews and Luke the more universal elements in his message.

(v) When parallel passages are studied in detail we can see why Matthew and Luke have altered Mark but no reasons why the reverse process should have taken place. Mark's account of a particular event is often the longest and the most vivid and lifelike; the narratives in Matthew and Luke are shortened versions of this.

Mark's style is rough-and-ready, sometimes with grammatical slips and peculiar Greek constructions. The other writers substituted more correct Greek and smoother expressions or constructions, or they altered Markan words which they considered would not be understood or appreciated by their readers. Some of Mark's phrases suggest blame on the disciples for their foolishness or fear or lack of faith, while other passages imply a limitation of Jesus' powers. The language in such places has been altered, especially in Matthew, in order to remove such suspicions. In all these ways, Mark's Gospel is a primary source for our knowledge of Jesus' work; the others are secondary witnesses.

The argument is cumulative and is based on extensive and exact study of the text of the three Gospels. Each of the points mentioned here can be supported by reference to parallel passages.[1] One result of this conclusion about the priority of Mark is to emphasise the supreme importance of this book and the value and authority which were evidently assigned to it within a few years of its composition.

The only passages in Mark which have no parallel in Matthew or Luke are:

i. 1; iii. 20–21; iv. 26–29; vii. 3–4, 32–37; viii. 22–26; ix. 29, 48–49; xiii. 33–37; xiv. 51–52.

This matter consists of small sections of teaching or comment, the incident of the youth in Gethsemane, one parable (the growing seed) and two healing acts (a deaf stammerer and a blind man).

---

[1] For the evidence from such parallel passages, the reader is referred to the author's *The Synoptic Gospels* (Macmillan, 1960) or *A Critical Introduction to the Gospels* (Macmillan, 1955).

THE NATURE OF THE BOOK

The English word 'gospel' comes from two Anglo-Saxon words, *god* and *spel*, meaning good story. It is used as a translation of the Greek word *euaggelion*, the Latin for which is *evangelium*, which has come into our language in such words as 'evangelist' and 'evangelism'. The Christian 'gospel'—the good news of the coming of Christ, his message and his work—is thus a message which is to be proclaimed and at first did not mean a book at all. The Greek word was in common use in the Roman world to indicate good tidings of various kinds —for instance an announcement about the release of prisoners—and the visit of a Roman emperor to a province was described officially as 'good news' (*euaggelia*). It was also used, together with the cognate verb (to proclaim good news), in the Septuagint (the Greek translation of the Old Testament, made in the third century B.C., generally referred to as the LXX) to denote good news from God as declared by prophets. The prophet of the exile in Babylon spoke of the man 'who tells good tidings to Jerusalem', the good news being that the period of exile and tribulation was coming to an end (Isa. xl. 9), while a later prophet declared that he himself had been anointed or commissioned to 'preach good news to the poor', the 'day of the Lord's favour', when God would deliver the faithful from their afflictions (Isa. lxi. 1).

It was this use in the Old Testament which would be particularly in mind for the early Christians when they described their message as *euaggelion*. Paul used the term when speaking of his own work, referring to 'the gospel which I preach' (Gal. ii. 2) and to 'my gospel' and 'our gospel', associating with him other missionaries who

were engaged in the same proclamation. This is the
meaning of the word in the opening paragraph of Mark:
'The beginning of the gospel of Jesus Christ' (i. 1). This
is a 'heading' to the book and Mark starts his account
of Jesus' work by saying that he came into Galilee
'preaching the gospel of God' (i. 14)—the good news of
the coming or presence of the kingdom of God.

Later on, when a number of books had been written
giving an account of this 'gospel', they were distinguished as 'the good news according to . . .' and the
term Gospel came to be applied to the book itself. So
we speak of Mark's Gospel, Luke's Gospel, the Gospel
of Peter or of Thomas (later works, outside the New
Testament).

The Gospels cannot be classified according to any of
the usual categories of literature. Mark's book is not a
biography of Jesus, for there are many activities of his
and aspects of his life and work of which it tells us
nothing. Neither was it an account intended for future
generations; the writer had in mind only his own contemporaries and had no thought of providing for centuries to come, for he probably held the current view
that the end of the world would happen soon. We
should be more accurate if we thought of it as an extensive tract or pamphlet. It was a proclamation of good
news, intended to meet a particular situation in the first
century. The remarkable fact is that it has transcended
that situation and is still found to be of value and
inspiration.

Before the 'Gospels' there was thus a 'gospel'. We
can discern what that gospel was from the speeches
which are recorded in the Acts of the Apostles and from
the letters of Paul. It centred in the proclamation of the
coming of Jesus. The preachers declared that history

had led up to that event and they considered the Old Testament story as a preparation for the gospel. They stated that the messianic age had been inaugurated by the work of Jesus and the era would be closed with the triumph of the cause of God. The proclamation would therefore have to include some account of the life and teaching of Jesus. Only brief reference is made to this in the speeches of Christian preachers as recorded in the Acts (for these are inevitably only summaries of what was actually spoken) and in the letters of Paul and others; it is to the four Gospels that we turn for fuller information.

The story of Jesus was not written down, systematically at any rate, for some time. Mark's book was probably produced about A.D. 65, a generation after the crucifixion. There are three main reasons why the narrative was not immediately committed to writing:

(i) The early Christians were not literary people. Paul reminded his converts that their ranks included 'not many wise according to worldly standards, not many powerful, not many of noble birth' (1 Cor. i. 26), and most of the Christians of the first century would not have had the ability or the time to set out a written account. Writing a book was then a long and expensive business, as it had to be done on sheets or a roll of papyrus and all written by hand. Very few people could afford to possess books of their own and the early Christians, most of them busy working people and some of them slaves, were not accustomed to handling or writing books.

(ii) Even if they had had the opportunity, it is doubtful if they would have seen the necessity for a written account, for future preservation. The urgent matter for them was for everyone to hear the gospel, especially in view of the expectation that the 'end of the age' was near. They thought that Christ would appear and would bring about the resurrection and judgment, ushering in a new age. Paul himself thought at one time that his generation would be the last. The message had to be delivered to as many as possible, before it was too late. There would be no point in setting it down for the benefit of future generations.

(iii) The story could in any case be remembered without being written down. Among the Jews the rabbis used to instruct their pupils orally; their teaching was learnt by heart, without any written notes. This was the practice also in Roman schools, where the pupils would repeat the matter after the teacher until it was perfectly known. Jesus himself probably adopted some such method in instructing his disciples. They in turn would pass on the teaching and would tell of incidents at which they themselves had been present. Their hearers would be able to relate them to others and in the Christian meetings the teaching of Jesus and the stories about him would be repeated. All this was possible because people in the ancient world had very good memories. This is still the case in places in the modern world where people do not rely on the written word as much as we do.

THE ORAL PERIOD

During this time the tradition was necessarily frag-mentary. Nobody would remember the whole of the story, but separate incidents and parts of Jesus' teaching would be recorded by different individuals. As these were repeated, there would be a tendency for the stories to assume something like a regular pattern or form. We can see traces of this in the Gospels, for the narratives there can be classified in a number of different types. Some of them have their chief interest in a statement by Jesus, some are stories of healing, while others are about the companions of Jesus. The study of these 'forms' is called Form Criticism (or Form History, from the German word *Formgeschichte*, for German scholars were the pioneers in this study), to distinguish it from Textual Criticism (study of the text in manuscripts and translations) and Source Criticism (study of the sources or materials used by an author). We are able to place the material found in our Gospels (and this study applies particularly to Mark, as it was the first one to be written) in roughly four categories, which correspond to types of oral material in circulation among the first generation of Christians:

(i) Stories which are linked with some saying of Jesus, with which the account concludes. Martin Dibelius called these Paradigms or models, but Vincent Taylor's term, Pronouncement-Stories, is commonly used. Many of the short narratives in Mark seem to have their climax in a statement by Jesus. A clear instance is the story of the question about tribute to the Romans (Mark xii. 13–17), which concludes with the pronouncement by Jesus: 'Render to Caesar what is due to Caesar and to God what is due to God.' Other typical instances are: Jesus and outcasts (ii. 15–17); the question of fasting (ii. 18–20); the treatment of the Sabbath (ii. 23–27); Jesus' true relations (iii. 31–35); the demand for a sign (viii. 11–12); the exorcist (ix. 38–40); the question of divorce (x. 2–9); the reception of children (x. 13–15); the rich man (x. 17–22); the question of resurrection (xii. 18–27); the chief commandment (xii. 28–31); the widow's mites (xii. 41–44).

Many of these topics were of interest not only to the

people to whom Jesus actually spoke but also to the early Christians, who were uncertain about the relation of Christianity to Jewish institutions like fasting and the Sabbath, their attitude towards the Roman rule or towards 'outsiders' and children and rich people. A story told about Jesus and how he had pronounced when faced with a similar problem would be recalled when such topics were discussed; the narrative was remembered primarily for the sake of the saying to which it led. This is not of course to say that the story itself had not great interest and value.

(ii) Stories which told of the power of Jesus in healing people and in performing mighty works. The miracle-stories (a term frequently used for such narratives) which occur in Mark are: the possessed man in the synagogue (i. 23–28); Peter's mother-in-law (i. 29–31); the leper (i. 40–45); the paralytic (ii. 1–12); the with-. ered hand (iii. 1–6); the storm on the lake (iv. 35–41); the Gerasene madman (v. 1–20); Jairus' daughter (v. 22–23, 35–43); the woman with haemorrhage (v. 24–34); the feeding of five thousand (vi. 35–44); the voyage across the lake (vi. 45–52); the Syro-Phoenician woman's daughter (vii. 24–30); the deaf stammerer (vii. 32–37); the feeding of four thousand (viii. 1–9); the blind man at Bethsaida (viii. 22–26); the epileptic son (ix. 17–29); blind Bartimaeus (x. 46–52); the fig-tree (xi. 12–14, 20–21).

Many of these stories in Mark follow the same 'pattern'. There is first a statement of the disease or incapacity; then follows an appeal to Jesus by the sufferer or his friends. He makes his response, often in a question or a command; then comes the cure. Afterwards there is a general word of comment—exclamations of wonder from the crowd or criticism from his opponents. Such stories would be of value in the Christian assembly and also to missionaries in speaking to heathen people, as demonstrations of the power of Jesus. These people would be familiar with tales of marvels in pagan religions, but in contrast to these the narratives in the Gospels are soberly told and all the more striking because of their reticence.

(iii) Stories about people who were associated with Jesus or biographical sketches of Jesus himself. In these cases there is generally a fuller description of the circumstances than in the other stories. Most of these are found in Luke but there are the following narratives of this type in Mark: the baptism of Jesus (i. 9–11); his temptations (i. 12–13); the call of the disciples (i. 16–20); the call of Levi (ii. 14); Jesus' visit to Nazareth (vi. 1–6); the mission of the twelve (vi. 7–13); the death of John the baptist (vi. 21–29); Caesarea Philippi (viii. 27–33); the transfiguration (ix. 2–8); the anointing at Bethany (xiv. 3–9); the entombment of Jesus (xv. 42–46).

We must not imagine that these three types of narrative form hard-and-fast categories, for the types sometimes overlap and it is difficult to say where a particular incident would be best placed. Thus the story of Bartimaeus (x. 46–52) might be classed as a biographical-story, since the man's name is mentioned, or as a miracle-story, since he was cured. The cure of Peter's mother-in-law (i. 29–31) could also belong to either of these categories. The anointing at Bethany (xiv. 3–9) might be claimed as a pronouncement-story, since it ends with a saying of Jesus. We use these categories to help us to classify the material and to see more clearly the interests of the early Christians and their motives in preserving the oral traditions.

(iv) The teaching of Jesus, in sayings and parables. Just as the sayings of the rabbis were treasured by their pupils and repeated and discussed, so the words of Jesus were remembered and passed on to others. Some of his sayings were necessarily connected with a particular time or place. The statement that a prophet has no honour among his own people naturally fits into the situation at Nazareth (vi. 1–6), and the pronouncement about rendering to Caesar is obviously related to the occasion on which Pharisees and Herodians asked a question about this (xii. 13–17). But many of Jesus' sayings and parables have no definite time or place necessarily associated with them; these were probably repeated among the first Christians as detached utterances and we cannot be at all sure on what occasion they were spoken originally. When we turn to the other two Synoptic Gospels and compare them with each other or with Mark, we find indeed quite frequently that two writers do not agree about the time or place of a saying of Jesus. Parables which are grouped together in one Gospel are found separately in another. Jesus' teaching was evidently to a large extent remembered in a somewhat fragmentary form; it was left to the compiler of a written account to set it out in order. Thus Mark put together a section about parables, as typical of Jesus' teaching by this method (iv. 1–32; the only other parable in Mark is that of the vineyard, xii. 1ff.). He similarly brought together in ix. 39–50 a number of sayings that might have been uttered on almost any occasion or indeed on many different occasions.

There must also have been many sayings which were not written down and so have been lost. Some of them have been discovered on papyrus fragments found in Egypt. One such statement would have perished if Paul had not quoted it and Luke recorded it in the Acts—'It is more blessed to give than to receive' (Acts xx. 35).

THE WRITING OF THE GOSPEL

All this material was thus in circulation in the early Church before the writing of the first Gospel. The episodes of Jesus' life were told and retold as occasion demanded; the sayings and parables were recited. But we must not imagine that at a particular date the 'oral period' came to an end and henceforth disciples relied solely on written accounts. The two periods necessarily overlapped. A collection of Jesus' sayings was probably made within twenty years of the crucifixion and possibly some of the incidents were also written down. But such ma‘erial would be only fragmentary. No attempt seems to have been made at a connected account of Jesus' work from its beginning to its end, until Mark's Gospel appeared.

The writer of this Gospel was thus not an author or biographer in the modern sense. He was rather an editor or compiler, making use of material already to a large extent familiar to his readers. He had to link together the separate episodes, introducing them with notes of time and place and supplying a connection with preceding matter. Sometimes he grouped together material which had a similar theme (e.g. the conflict-stories of ii. 1 to iii. 6; the challenges to Jesus in xi. 27 to xii. 27) and sometimes compiled a series of parables or sayings, or made use of a collection which had already been compiled (the parables in iv. 1–32; the sayings in ix. 39–50; apocalyptic matter in chap. xiii). He added comments about Jesus' method of teaching (iv. 33) or a summary of his work (vi. 53–56) or explanatory notes to help readers unfamiliar with the situation in Palestine (vii. 3–4).

There were a number of reasons why the oral period came to an end and the Christians had to rely on the written accounts of the 'good news'. The original apostles were going. James was the first of the twelve to be put to death, about A.D. 42 (Acts xii. 2). It is probable that Peter and Paul were executed during the persecution of the Christians in Rome in the reign of Nero in A.D. 64–65. Other apostles would be scattered in different parts of the world and were not available with their first-hand reminiscences of the life of Jesus. There was also the danger that the story would be distorted because of failing memories and the oral account would be no longer reliable. It would have to be preserved in a more tangible form if it was not to become a tradition comparable to the legends of Greek and Roman religions, with no definite historical foundation. Written accounts would also be required for reading in Church worship. The early Christians followed the practice of Jews in their synagogues, in having readings from the Old Testament, and there would arise the need for a written account of Jesus' ministry which could be put alongside this.

So the telling of the stories and sayings gradually ceased and the written accounts took their place. Mark's book was thus a pioneer work, for it was used later by the writers of Luke and Matthew as the basis of their more extended accounts of Jesus' work and teaching.

THE MATERIALS USED BY MARK

Mark obviously made use of the oral material, which has been studied above. His was apparently the first attempt to relate this in consecutive order and to combine narrative and teaching in one complete book. Many of the accounts in the Gospel still show the 'form' which they took when they were still being told by word of mouth.

Early Church writers all agree that one authority behind Mark's writing was the apostle Peter. This tradition goes back to the words of Papias, who was bishop of Hierapolis, in Asia Minor, about A.D. 130. As reported by Eusebius, the Church historian (about 325), Papias quotes 'the Elder' (or 'Presbyter') as saying: 'Mark, having become the interpreter of Peter, wrote down accurately all that he remembered of the things said and done by the Lord, but not however in order. For neither did he hear the Lord nor did he follow him but afterwards [attached himself] to Peter, who adapted his teaching to the needs [of the moment— or: of his hearers], but not as though he were drawing up a connected account of the Lord's sayings. So then Mark made no mistake in thus recording some things as he remembered them, for he made it his one care to omit nothing that he had heard and to make no false statement in them.'

The statement that Mark became the 'interpreter' of Peter has sometimes been taken to mean that Mark's task was to translate Peter's message, delivered in his native Aramaic, into the common Greek when he was preaching to Gentiles. But Peter would almost certainly be bilingual and would need no interpreter in this sense. It is more likely that Papias meant that Mark was a kind of secretary to Peter and expounded or interpreted his ideas to others, in much the same way as John Mark had acted formerly as 'attendant' or 'assistant' to Paul and Barnabas (Acts xiii. 5).

Most students of Mark have concluded that there is
Petrine matter in the Gospel and that the authority of
the apostle lies in some measure behind the book. A
curious feature is that the disciples in general and Peter
in particular are often treated in this book very harshly.
They are shown to be dull, not understanding Jesus'
words (iv. 14; vi. 52; viii. 18, 21; ix. 32), distrusting and
rebuking Jesus (iv. 38) and arguing with him (v. 31),
quarrelling among themselves (ix. 33–34) and demanding their own advancement (x. 35–37) and deserting
Jesus in his hour of greatest need (xiv. 40, 50). Peter
brings upon himself a rebuke in severe terms (viii. 33),
makes foolish suggestions (ix. 5–6), calls attention to
himself (x. 28), draws unwarranted conclusions (xi. 21),
boasts in extravagant terms (xiv. 29, 31), falls asleep
instead of keeping guard (xiv. 37) and denies, with
curses, all knowledge of Jesus (xiv. 71). In spite of this,
there is a special message for him at the end (xvi. 7). It
has been generally concluded that this portrait of Peter
arises from the fact that the stories were told by himself,
in all humility, and that Mark faithfully recorded his
failures and the weaknesses of his fellow apostles. On
the other hand, it might indicate that the writer had a
prejudice against the twelve and a particular spite
against Peter and deliberately portrayed him in this
fashion.

We must not, however, place too much weight upon
Papias' words about Mark's dependence on Peter.
Much in the Gospel seems to embody a general Christian tradition rather than the personal reminiscences of
one man. There are traits which do not suggest an
eyewitness; there are two accounts of a feeding of a
crowd (vi. 34–44; viii. 1–10) which seem to be variants
of the same incident. This suggests two different

sources. There is confusion in some places about the geography of Galilee and northern Palestine in general (see the notes on vi. 45, 53; vii. 31), which suggests that the writer had not at hand an eyewitness to whom he could refer for more accurate details.

It is also probable that some of the teaching found in Mark was already in written form. The parables in iv. 3–34 may have been already collected together, as well as the sayings in ix. 41–50, and a written document may underlie the apocalyptic matter in chap. xiii. The sayings on ritual cleanness in vii. 1–23 may already have been written down and connected in this somewhat artificial way and Mark merely reproduced them as he found them. In general, we may conclude that the material of the Gospel consisted of the matter circulating in the oral period, that he had the authority of Peter for much, but not all, of what he wrote, that some of the narratives and teaching of Jesus were already in written form, but no attempt had been made to set out in a systematic arrangement an account of Jesus' ministry from beginning to end. This study thus reinforces the pioneer nature of Mark's work.

THE CHARACTERISTICS OF THE BOOK

Mark's Gospel is the most vivid of all the four, in its portrayal of Jesus. It has many graphic details often omitted by the later writers. Mark describes Jesus as expressing strong emotion when approached by a leper (i. 41, 43), as regarding his opponents with anger (iii. 5), as sleeping on the cushion provided for passengers in a fisherman's boat (iv. 38), as being surprised at the unbelief of his fellow-townsmen (vi. 6), as taking little children in the crook of his arm (ix. 36; x. 16), as regarding a rich man with affection (x. 21), as being distressed at his impending fate (xiv. 33–34) and as refusing to answer Pilate's questions (xv. 5). There is an impression of speed and urgency; the writer goes from one incident to another with very little 'padding' between. He is fond of the historic present tense, using it 151 times to produce a vivid impression in his narrative. The book opens abruptly; Jesus appears, without introduction, at i. 9; and (if xvi. 8 is the conclusion of the book as Mark penned it) it finishes just as abruptly. The style of the Greek is rough and the grammar occasionally faulty, by strict standards.

Papias said that Mark wrote 'accurately but not in order'. This sounds somewhat disparaging but we do not know in what sense he found Mark without 'order'. Some have concluded that he was comparing Mark's chronological scheme with that in some other book. This may have been the fourth Gospel, which certainly gives a different 'order' in many respects, or the Gospel of Matthew, where the teaching of Jesus is collected and reproduced in five blocks, although the basic narrative is Mark's. Others have taken the word to refer to literary arrangement; the comparison with Matthew is more relevant here. Another view is that the book was compiled to provide a series of readings in church services and Papias was criticising the arrangement because it could not be used in the churches with which he was familiar. All these suggestions, however, may be reading too much into a simple statement and Papias may have been merely referring in quite general terms to the lack of connection between incidents in the Gospel, which is plain to any discerning reader, and suggesting that they might have been arranged in a better sequence.

Mark presents four aspects of the life and person of Jesus:

(i) As a man. Mark is most frank in the portrayal of Jesus' human limitations. He speaks of him as asking questions, in order to gain information (v. 30; ix. 16, 21), as unable to heal in certain circumstances (vi. 5), as using material means to cure people (vii. 33; viii. 23), as refusing to be called good (x. 18) and as being worried and distressed (xiv. 33–34). But his authority is also stressed; from the first it is noticed by the people— the authority of his words (i. 22) and of his deeds (i. 27; ii. 12). Jesus gives commands—to sick people (i. 43; ii. 11; iii. 3, 5; v. 19), to the demons (i. 25; v. 8; ix. 25), to disciples (i. 17; vi. 7; viii. 30; cf. x. 21; x. 49) and to his opponents (xi. 15–16; xii. 15). His life is portrayed as one of intense activity. Twice Mark says that Jesus was so busy or engrossed that there was no opportunity to have a meal (iii. 20; vi. 31).

(ii) As the Messiah. This Hebrew word (the Greek for which is 'Christ') means literally 'anointed'. In the Old Testament it was applied, as an adjective, to kings and to prophets. It was not applied to a *future* king. But there was, particularly towards the end of the Old Testament period, a general expectation of a time of righteousness and prosperity to be brought about by God himself. This was often spoken of by the prophets. Some writers also referred to a righteous kingdom, wherein God's faithful worshippers would be vindicated and his will would be carried out. From this it was but natural to think of a righteous king, to reign in the future and act as God's agent. He was thought of as belonging to the royal line of David. When, however, this line ceased, with the fall of Jerusalem to the Babylonians in 586 B.C., the future king came to be considered as an idealised David. He was to conquer his enemies and rule righteously by might. There is no suggestion in the Old Testament that he was regarded as divine and he is never actually called the Messiah.

The idea of a future king became more defined in the period between the Old Testament and the time of Jesus, especially in the apocalyptic works. The writers of these thought that God would intervene in the midst of calamity and tragedy and establish his righteous kingdom. The future king comes definitely to be called the Messiah. The hope of political freedom, when the Jews were under the rule of a foreign power such as the Greek kings or, later, the Romans, was associated with the expectation of a divine deliverance. The Messiah, as a descendant of David, would restore the monarchy. His expected reign would be a vindication of the Jews; this was sometimes interpreted in narrow, nationalistic terms. But there were some who had a wider conception of God's purpose and remembered that in the Old Testament there were passages which spoke of his care for all men and one picture at least of a king who came not as a warrior but in peace (Zech. ix. 9–10).

The 'heading' of Mark's book is: 'The good news of Jesus the Messiah' (i. 1). His messiahship, however, is a secret which is known to the demons (iii. 11; cf. i. 24, 34) but not perceived by men. They think of him as John the baptist or Elijah or a prophet (viii. 28). Jesus himself does not proclaim who he is; he seems to have become aware of it at his baptism, where a voice from heaven quoted 'Thou art my son' from Ps. ii. 7. The first acknowledgment of him as Messiah by any man was made at Caesarea Philippi (viii. 29) and Jesus immediately enjoined silence on those who heard Peter say this. The first time he was publicly hailed as Messiah was at Jericho, when Bartimaeus called him 'son of David' (x. 47). Messiahship may have been hinted at when Jesus entered Jerusalem on a colt (xi. 9–10) but the first time that Jesus himself claimed this was at his trial, in answer to a question from the high priest (xiv. 61–62). The priests who mocked him on the cross remembered this (xv. 32), but the charge which Pilate had to investigate was that of being king of the Jews (xv. 2, 26), which had political implications. The book closes with the verdict of a Roman centurion, that this man was God's son (xv. 39)—meant no doubt by him in a pagan way but interpreted by Mark's readers as an acknowledgment of the messiahship which had been portrayed through the book.

It is plain that Jesus' interpretation of this was far different from the ideas of his contemporaries. Immediately after Peter's acknowledgment, he began to speak of rejection, suffering and death (viii. 31). This conception is not to be found in the Old Testament or in contemporary Judaism. But the term used here is not Messiah but Son of Man.

(iii) As Son of Man. This term had a long history before it appeared in the Gospels. In Hebrew and Aramaic 'son of man' meant simply 'man'. The writer of Ps. viii. 4 asks 'What is man?' and adds the parallel question 'And the son of man?' (cf. Ps. lxxx. 17; Isa. lvi. 2; Job xvi. 21; xxv. 6; xxxv. 8). Used in the plural 'sons of men' meant human beings (Ps. xii. 8; lxxxix. 47). The prophet Ezekiel is addressed many times by God as 'son of man'; this may imply that in some way Ezekiel was being considered as representative of his fellow-men. The author of the book of Daniel, after picturing as wild animals the great empires which had in turn oppressed the Jews, saw 'one like a son of man' coming to God, to receive 'dominion and glory and a kingdom' (Dan. vii. 13–14). He was writing during the persecution of the faithful Jews by the Greek–Syrian king, Antiochus Epiphanes, in 168 B.C., and sought to bring comfort and encouragement to his fellow-countrymen by declaring that this comparatively puny figure, in contrast to the beasts, would reign in triumph after the temporary victory of the great empires, for the 'figure like a man' represented 'the saints of the Most High' (Dan. vii. 18, 22). But this triumph would be gained not by force and might of arms but by patient endurance and loyalty to their God.

The idea was developed in later apocalyptic works but the figure became personal and was referred to as 'the Son of Man' or 'The Man', who would bring in the messianic age. He was an 'Elect One' who would come with God for the judgment of the world, to condemn the wicked and to reign over the righteous. We cannot say definitely whether or not the Son of Man was regarded in the first century A.D. as the same as the Messiah.

The Son of Man is mentioned thirteen times in Mark's Gospel. In two places the term comes early in the narrative, in ways that have no parallel elsewhere (ii. 10 and ii. 28. The notes on these passages deal with the meaning there). Apart from these, all the occurrences are after the acknowledgment of Jesus as Messiah at Caesarea Philippi (viii. 27ff.). In three of these there is the conventional idea of the Son of Man as a figure of glory (viii. 38; xiii. 26; xiv. 62). But in all other cases the Son of Man is spoken of as one who would suffer humiliation, would give himself in service to men but would ultimately be triumphant. There are three predictions of what would happen to him at Jerusalem

(viii. 31; ix. 31; x. 33; cf. ix. 9, 12). The Son of Man is said to suffer betrayal into the hands of his enemies (xiv. 21, 41) and to act as a servant and even to give his life (x. 45). This picture of one who achieves his victory not by force but by patient suffering is reminiscent of the writings of an unknown prophet of the exile, where four poems about the Servant of Yahweh are incorporated in Isa. xlii, xlix, l, lii–liii.

(iv) As a teacher and preacher. The note of authority in Jesus' words has already been observed (e.g. i. 22). Many of the pronouncement-stories, which have their climax in a statement by Jesus, are found in Mark. Much of his teaching is thus related to specific occasions or to questions which were put to him by friends or opponents. More connected teaching is given in the group of parables in iv. 3–34, the sayings in ix. 41–50 and the apocalyptic matter in chap. xiii.

The Author of the Gospel

All the four Gospels are anonymous; only in the prologue to Luke (i. 1–4) is the first person singular used and even this does not give us the name of the author. The titles usually given to the Gospels were added later, when manuscripts were copied by scribes and some distinction had to be made between the four accounts. To find out the author of a book we have to follow two lines of investigation: external evidence (the views of other people, such as the remarks of early writers about the book), and internal evidence (hints supplied by the book itself).

The earliest reference to this Gospel is contained in the words of Papias, which have been quoted above (p. 21). This statement is not derived directly from Papias'

writings, for these have perished, but from a report by
the church historian Eusebius (about 325), who wrote
that Papias quoted a figure in the Church of his own
time whom he called 'the Elder' (or 'the Presbyter').
About 180 Irenaeus, bishop of Lyons, stated that 'Mark
transmitted in writing the things that Peter used to
preach'. From that time it was the accepted view that
this Gospel was written by one called Mark.

It is generally assumed that this Mark was the same
as the one (the only man of that name) mentioned in
the Acts and some of Paul's letters. He is introduced
first as 'John named Mark', John being his Jewish
name and Marcus an added Roman one; Peter is stated
to have gone to the house of his mother, where the
disciples had met together, after his release from prison
(Acts xii. 12). He later accompanied Paul and Barnabas
to Antioch in Syria (xii. 25) and from there the three
set out on a missionary journey (xiii. 5), Mark acting as
the attendant or assistant of the other two. When they
departed from Cyprus, Mark returned to Jerusalem
(xiii. 13)—why, we do not know. He was later the cause
of a quarrel between Paul and Barnabas and the latter
went with him again to Cyprus (xv. 36–37). He evidently
became later reconciled to Paul, who referred to him
as Barnabas' cousin (Col. iv. 10; Philem. 24; 2 Tim. iv.
11). It is apparently the same man who is referred to in
1 Pet. v. 13 as being with the apostle in Babylon (which
probably means Rome).

The evidence of the book itself bears out the view that
it was written by John Mark. The style of writing
suggests one who was not a polished author in Hellenistic Greek. He knew the language and could write quite
forcefully in it but it was not his native tongue. If John
Mark was from Jerusalem, he would have Aramaic as

his language at home, but would also be able to speak the common Greek which would be needed on his travels. But he would probably think and express himself more naturally in Aramaic and there are expressions in the Gospel which suggest that Aramaic phrases and idioms have been translated into Greek in the writer's mind before he put them down.

The book does not suggest the work of an eyewitness, although there are features which suggest the influence of such a man. The only place where there is a hint of personal reminiscence is in the strange incident at Jesus' arrest in Gethsemane (xiv. 51–52) but it is not certain that this refers to Mark himself; the youth may have been rather his informant about the events which took place. The writer shows himself to be vague about the geography of northern Palestine. He often does not state which part of Galilee he is referring to (e.g. vi. 31) and the company wanders to and from 'the other side' of the lake in a very confusing way (vi. 45; cf. v. 1, 21). The disciples start from an unnamed place to go to Bethsaida (vi. 45) but they arrive at Gennesaret, in a different direction (vi. 53); they eventually arrive at Bethsaida considerably later (viii. 22) but in the meantime they have visited Phoenicia (vii. 24) and made a journey back to Galilee by a very peculiar route through Decapolis (vii. 31). John Mark would be familiar with Judea rather than with Galilee, and probably did not know northern Palestine well.

The roughness of the book may also be regarded as supporting the traditional authorship, for it accords with the character of John Mark as portrayed in the Acts—probably impulsive and somewhat unreliable but sufficiently attractive to be supported by his cousin Barnabas and later to become reconciled to Paul himself. One would expect him to write a book such as this, with all its faults yet with its special attraction and charm.

THE DATE OF THE GOSPEL

If the book was written by John Mark of the Acts, the date must obviously be within the apostolic era. Papias says nothing about this but his statement suggests that Peter was no longer at hand to supervise Mark's account of his preaching. Peter was probably put to death in the persecution which followed the fire of Rome in A.D. 64–65. An early prologue attached to the Gospel (160–180) states that after the death of Peter Mark wrote the Gospel in Italy. Irenaeus (180) said that Mark set down his record after the deaths of Peter and Paul, while about the same time Clement of Alexandria stated that Mark wrote with the agreement of Peter himself while the apostle was still preaching in Rome.

The date usually accepted now is between 65 and 70, for the following reasons:

(i) The death of Peter in the persecution was probably one of the reasons which impelled Mark to take the work in hand. Others of the first disciples of Jesus were probably dead by this time also and the need was realised for a written account of the traditions which up to that time had been mainly transmitted orally.

(ii) A note of persecution and suffering is prominent in many parts of the book. Jesus warns his disciples about taking up a cross (viii. 34) and about drinking their own cup (x. 38f.). They must not be ashamed of him and his words (viii. 38) and are promised ample compensation for what they give up for his sake (x. 29f.). This emphasis would be of special encouragement to the Christians who were living in Rome at this time of trial.

(iii) There is a warning in xiii. 14 of 'an appalling horror' or 'profanation' ('the abomination of desolation'), 'standing where it [literally 'he'] ought not to be'. This was to be the signal for people in Judea to flee to the mountains, not stopping to return home to pick up their belongings. This well describes the situation of refugees when an invading army approaches and the reference to such a crisis in Judea points to the presence of the Roman forces when they laid siege to Jerusalem and eventually captured the city. They then entered the Temple courts and set the building on fire. The Jewish Christians had fled before this, however. The writers of the later Gospels took Mark's reference to be to these events, for Luke changed his words to 'when you see Jerusalem surrounded by armies' (Luke xxi. 20), while Matthew wrote of the 'abomination standing in the holy place' (Matt. xxiv. 15). This sacrilege in the Temple, parallel to the setting up of pagan altars by Antiochus Epiphanes in 168 B.C. (to which the quotation from Daniel referred), would be the presence of the Roman troops in the sacred courts of the Temple, for their standards dedicated to the divine Caesar were regarded as heathen symbols by the Jews. The statement in Mark appears to be studiously vague, as if he were not sure what form the sacrilege would take. If he had been writing after the fall of the city (in A.D. 70) he would surely have been more definite. The phrases suggest that the final siege had not yet begun—it lasted over two years—but he feared the worst, yet did not dare to be more precise about the nature of the horrors to come.

The place of writing is generally taken to be Rome,

although Antioch and Alexandria have been suggested.
It is certain that he wrote for Gentiles. When he quotes
Aramaic words of Jesus he translates them into Greek
for the benefit of his readers (v. 41; vii. 11, 34; xv. 22)
and goes out of his way to explain the Jewish practice of
ritual washing (vii. 3–4). There are also some Latin
words, in their Greek forms—legion (v. 9), denarius
(xii. 15), quadrans (xii. 42), praetorium (xv. 16) and
centurion (xv. 39)—but this is not decisive for Rome as
the place of writing, for these words were in regular use
in the Roman world. Early writers such as Irenaeus and
Clement say that the book was written at Rome. Peter
probably spent his last years at Rome and tradition said
that his influence was behind Mark. Mark is said to have
gone later to Alexandria and settled there and it is thus
possible that the book was written then.

THE STRUCTURE OF MARK'S GOSPEL

The account of Jesus' ministry in Mark (which is
followed in the main in Luke and Matthew) falls into
four well-defined periods:

I. *Jesus' work in Galilee* (i to vii. 23)

Following on the imprisonment of John the baptist,
Jesus taught and worked in Galilee, except for one brief
journey to the east of the lake (v. 1–20). There are four
aspects of his ministry here:

(a) His deeds. These consisted mainly of acts of
healing. As a consequence, he became popular with the
crowds but he often told people whom he cured to say
nothing about it (e.g. i. 21 to ii. 12; iii. 1–6; v. 1–43).
There were also three so-called 'nature miracles' (iv.
35–41; vi. 45–52; vi. 30–44).

(b) His teaching and preaching. The theme of this

was the kingdom of God (i. 15). The nature of the kingdom was explained in parables (iv. 1–33).

(c) The choice of twelve disciples. As was customary with eastern teachers, he chose a small company from the crowds which listened to him (iii. 13–19). On these he could concentrate and send them out on a preaching mission (vi. 7–13).

(d) Opposition. The religious authorities soon began to oppose Jesus. They represented orthodox Judaism and were disturbed at the authority with which he spoke and acted. They were also scandalised because of the free way in which he and his disciples treated the Jewish Laws, especially the regulations about the observance of the Sabbath and ritual washing. They also considered that he ignored the distinction between loyal and faithful Jews and 'sinners', people who did not observe strictly the Old Testament laws and the traditional practices (ii–iii; vii. 1–23). Their opposition did not arise from mere prejudice or blind obstinacy but from genuine regard for their religion and a desire to preserve its purity, however mistaken they were in the methods they adopted.

II. *Journeys in the north* (vii. 24 to ix. 50)

Jesus and the disciples visited Phoenicia, where a Greek woman's daughter was healed (vii. 24–30). Further journeys on the outskirts of Galilee followed (viii. 1–26). They went to the territory of Herod Philip (viii. 27 to ix. 29) and eventually got back to Capernaum (ix. 30–50).

III. *Journey towards Jerusalem* (x)

Travelling through Perea, Jesus received little children, challenged a rich man to leave all and follow him, and taught the ambitious disciples about true greatness, when they wished for the most important places. At Jericho he healed a blind man who called him Son of David (x. 46–52).

IV. *Last days in Jerusalem* (xi–xvi. 8)

Jesus entered Jerusalem and was acclaimed by the people. After he had cleared the Temple court of those who were making it into a market, he was challenged by the authorities of the Jews (xi–xii). Assisted by an offer from Judas, the priests plotted against him. Jesus and the disciples had a last meal together, which was followed by his arrest, trial before the Sanhedrin and the Roman procurator, and execution (xiv–xv). His body was put in a rock tomb, which some women visited early on Sunday morning, to be told by a young man that Jesus had risen and gone to Galilee. Mark's account breaks off abruptly with the women fleeing from the tomb in fear (xvi. 8).

DIFFERENT VIEWS OF THE BOOK

Students of Mark's Gospel have shown great divergence in their views of the nature of the book and of what the author's main intention was. The book is, as we have seen, primarily a declaration of good news— 'the gospel of Jesus the Messiah' (i. 1). The question which is further asked is: Can we discern any special emphasis which the writer wished to make or any interests which he had particularly in mind? Was there one dominating purpose when he wrote the book?

Mark has often been regarded as giving an outline of the historical ministry of Jesus, correct in its details of chronology and the order of events, preserving a genuine reminiscence of Peter. This outline is in the main followed by the other two Synoptic writers and was cited as evidence of careful planning and exact reporting on the part of Mark.

This 'Markan outline' gives first an account of Jesus' Galilean work, with stories of his preaching, healing acts and opposition from his enemies. Jesus decided not to trust the crowds but to concentrate on a few men, so he chose the twelve and sent them out to preach. On their return he wished for retirement for a while but was frustrated by the crowds which followed him, so he went to Phoenicia, but was known even there. So he proceeded to Herod Philip's territory, where he found out from the disciples what people thought of him and that they thought that he was the Messiah. Shortly after this, the journey to Jerusalem began, leading swiftly to a final clash with the Jewish authorities and, after a week of controversy, to his arrest and crucifixion.

This scheme seems to give an intelligible and straightforward account of Jesus' work. But there are difficulties in accepting it fully as the only possible and reliable account. It is incomplete and inadequate chronologically; there is little indication in Mark's account of the time of most of the incidents and the only mention of season is the reference to the ripe ears of corn in ii. 23 and the green grass in vi. 39, and the fact that Jesus was crucified at the season of the Passover. But we have no clue whether two or more springtimes are indicated. Little time seems to be allowed in the narrative for Jesus to have become known throughout Galilee and even for his fame to have reached Phoenicia (vii. 24) and Jericho (x. 47). There are hints in the other Synoptics (quite apart from the fourth Gospel, which has a different chronological and geographical scheme

altogether) that Jesus had more than once appealed to
Jerusalem and also suggesting work in places in Galilee
which are not mentioned in Mark or only very briefly.
Further, when Jesus reached Jerusalem, there is no
indication in Mark how long it was before the Passover;
it has indeed been pointed out that some of the details
of his entry into the city suggest the feast of Tabernacles
rather than Passover. The only indication of time in this
period is the note that the plot against Jesus was
planned two days before the Passover (xiv. 1).

It is thus uncertain whether we can rely upon Mark
for an adequate or reliable chronological outline of
Jesus' work. It is doubtful if Mark would have been
interested in providing this, in any case. But this is not
to say that his outline is not dependable at all. It does
present a true picture of Jesus' Galilean work and his
last days in Jerusalem. But we cannot claim more for it
than the writer intended. It is not possible to say of an
incident or a section of teaching that it occurred at a
particular place at a particular stage in the ministry.

The Form Critics go to the other extreme and tend to
regard Mark as a kind of patchwork. It embodies the
oral material which was available for the author but he
had only fragmentary and disconnected episodes or
sayings. They hold that the connections between para-
graphs and the setting for the teaching are entirely
artificial and the work of Mark himself, and that no
outline of the ministry of Jesus was preserved in tradition or can be recovered by us in our study of the
Gospels. The force of this view relies upon the fact that
the Gospel is certainly a collection of episodes and
there are abrupt transitions from one paragraph to
another; Mark also has obviously collected and arranged, sometimes somewhat artificially, similar mater-

ial, in incidents or in teaching. Nevertheless there is definite progression in Mark's arrangement: the ministry of Jesus begins after his baptism by John; his main work is done in Galilee: thence he travels to Jerusalem, where the opposition reaches its climax. We get the impression that this progressive scheme is not merely the writer's creation, but that he was following a tradition and arranged the material within this historical framework.

The view of the Gospel as a series of disconnected episodes without any certain or trustworthy connection thus goes too far in the other direction, as a revolt against the rigidity of the 'Markan hypothesis'.

Mark's Gospel is often regarded today primarily as a theological work. It is said that our first efforts must be directed towards discovering and understanding his theological point of view; then his treatment of the story of Jesus becomes plainer. One of the first attempts to expound Mark in this way was that of W. Wrede in 1901 (*The Messianic Secret in the Gospels*). He held that Mark's Gospel was written in order to account for the fact that the early Christians proclaimed Jesus as the Messiah. He declared that Jesus himself had not claimed this and he was not accepted as Messiah until after the resurrection; it was this event (however we may interpret it) which caused the disciples to realise who Jesus was. Wrede held that Jesus was recognised by the demons and later by an intimate band of disciples, but he told them to keep it a secret until after the resurrection. This is indeed plainly stated in Mark. But Wrede urged that the 'messianic secret' was an artificial construction of Mark himself; so the Gospel was not to be regarded as historically reliable in its presentation of Jesus, but as the exposition of a theological point of view.

R. H. Lightfoot, in 1935 (*History and Interpretation in the Gospels*), emphasised that theological interpretation was to be found not only in the fourth Gospel (as was generally agreed) but in the Synoptics also, including the Gospel which was frequently regarded as the most reliable historically and most free from theological bias. It was consequently impossible for us to be certain we could 'see Jesus' as his contemporaries did; we could view him only through the eyes of the evangelists. From another point of view, J. H. Ropes held that Mark was written to explain how it was that the Jewish Messiah suffered death at the hands of his own people. The book is 'a kind of theological pamphlet—a discussion of a problem in the form of a dramatic historical sketch' (*The Synoptic Gospels*, p. 12).

Others have considered that the writer of Mark was concerned to expound the views of Paul. The apostle to the Gentiles deals in Rom. ix–xi with the problem of the Jews' rejection of the Messiah. B. W. Bacon held that the counterpart to Paul's discussion is the theory in Mark of the 'hardening' of the disciples' hearts (iv. 13; vi. 52; viii. 17). This view has not been generally favoured. There are certainly some phrases used in Mark which have parallels in Paul's writings (e.g. Mark x. 45) but the influence of the apostle was probably so great among the Gentile churches in the first century that it is only to be expected that some of his ideas and terminology would be the common property of all preachers.

A more recent attempt to understand Mark in this theological way is that of Austin Farrer, who holds that Mark's theological arrangement was cyclic. The narratives told in the early parts of the book 'prefigure' the later events of the Passion and resurrection. He holds that this restores the unity of the Gospel and makes it 'a profoundly consistent, complex act of thought'. The book is consequently arranged not on an historical basis but artificially, as determined by 'motives of Christian symbolism' (*A Study in St Mark*, pp. 7, 146).

The 'theological' view of Mark has arisen to a large extent as a reaction against the view of the book as presenting a portrait of the 'simple human Jesus', treated as a straightforward biography. It does seem plain now that much of the material in Mark was arranged by the writer himself and that doctrinal considerations did influence him in this. Without endorsing what we might consider the extravagances of some of the foregoing views, D. E. Nineham (in the Penguin commentary on Mark) emphasises that a 'Gospel' is inevitably the expression of a theology, since it sets out to portray and proclaim the works of Jesus the Messiah. Instead of reading the book as we would read a 'Life of Christ' produced in our own day, we must try to see its contents through the eyes of its first readers and consider the impact made on them. Mark was not writing for our generation, with its emphasis on factual knowledge and historical exactitude, but for his contemporaries and for people who were already believers in Jesus. He was showing them not only how Jesus of Nazareth lived and influenced men in his own day but also how Jesus the Christ would speak to them and how his teaching and actions could encourage them in their own circumstances and illuminate their problems.

There is thus much in the Gospel which does reflect the attitude of the first-century Christians towards Jesus, and the account is given a 'slant' which is obviously derived from this factor. But there is also much in the Gospel which clearly has little or no connection with a specifically theological purpose. Many of the incidents are surely related simply because the writer thought it worth while to preserve them and to give the accounts of the life and teaching of Jesus a more permanent form than they could ever have in the oral tradition.

This raises the question of the historical accuracy of the Gospel: how far are we entitled to consider it a reliable record of what happened in Palestine? The reader may be able to come to his own conclusion after making a study of the book. On the whole we may conclude that Jesus did the kind of things reported of him; he preached in the synagogues, taught the disciples, proclaimed the kingdom of God, spoke in parables, mixed with men and women and helped them and healed the sick. But we cannot be certain that he did these things exactly in the way that Mark reports them. Mark naturally wrote as a man of the first century and he was writing for people with a different background and different presuppositions from ours. His attitude towards Jesus' acts of power, for instance, was not that of a modern reporter or historian. We may find it necessary and indeed helpful to our understanding of a miracle to distinguish between the account as Mark gives it and the historical reality behind it; we may demand to know 'what actually happened'. Some attempt is made in this book to give different views about some of Jesus' acts. But for Mark an attempt to 'explain' a miracle would have had no relevance or significance. Similarly in recording Jesus' teaching, Mark was not concerned to reproduce this as a series of ethical maxims, as a guide for everyday conduct. All the features of Jesus' work—his teaching, his miracles, his dealings with the disciples—were for him and the early Christians aspects of Jesus' proclamation of the kingdom of God.

We have seen above that Mark's book represents a new type of literature. It is not a biography of Jesus of Nazareth in the sense in which such a book would be written today. His book is a 'gospel'—a record of the good news which was initially proclaimed by Jesus himself and which the early Church preached about him and the significance of his life among men.

PALESTINE

English Miles

0 5 10   20   30   40

SUMMARY OF CONTENTS OF THE GOSPEL

Chapter

I THE FIRST ACTIVITIES OF JESUS

The preaching of John the baptist (verses 1–8)
The baptism and temptation of Jesus (9–13)
Jesus' first preaching and call of disciples (14–20)
Jesus' first preaching in Capernaum (21–28)
The cure of Peter's mother-in-law and others (29–34)
A withdrawal by Jesus (35–39)
The healing of a leper (40–45)

II OPPOSITION TO JESUS

The healing of a paralysed man (verses 1–12)
The call of Levi and its sequel (13–17)
A question about fasting (18–22)
An incident in the cornfields (23–28)

III FURTHER CAUSES OF OPPOSITION AND MISUNDERSTANDING

The cure of a man's withered hand (verses 1–6)
Teaching by the lake (7–12)
The choice of twelve disciples (13–19)
The anxiety of Jesus' friends (20–21)
The accusation of Jesus' enemies (22–30)
Jesus' true family (31–35)

Chapter

IV   TEACHING BY PARABLES

The parable of the sower (verses 1–9)
The meaning of the parable (10–20)
Parabolic sayings (21–25)
The parable of the seed growing (26–29)
The parable of the mustard seed (30–32)
The use of parables (33–34)
A storm on the lake (35–41)

V   JESUS' WORKS OF POWER

The cure of a demoniac (verses 1–20)
Jairus' daughter (21–43)

VI   FURTHER GALILEAN ACTIVITIES

Jesus' visit to Nazareth (verses 1–6)
The mission of the twelve disciples (7–13)
The imprisonment and death of John the baptist (14–29)
The return of the disciples and the feeding of five thousand people (30–44)
The crossing of the lake (45–56)

VII   FURTHER OPPOSITION AND JOURNEYS OUTSIDE GALILEE

A dispute about scribal tradition (verses 1–23)
A visit to Phoenicia (24–30)
The cure of a deaf stammerer (31–37)

VIII   ON THE WAY TO CAESAREA PHILIPPI

The feeding of four thousand people (verses 1–10)
The demand for a sign (11–13)
The significance of the loaves (14–21)
The cure of a blind man (22–26)

Chapter

Jesus and the disciples near Caesarea Philippi (27–33)
Teaching on service and sacrifice (34–38; ix. 1)

IX   RETURN FROM THE NORTH TO CAPERNAUM

The transfiguration of Jesus (verses 2–13)
The cure of an epileptic (14–29)
Second statement of the Passion (30–32)
The child as an example (33–37)
The disciples and an exorcist (38–40)
Various sayings (41–50)

X   THE JOURNEY TOWARDS JERUSALEM

Teaching about divorce (verses 1–12)
The reception of children (13–16)
The rich man (17–31)
Third statement of the Passion (32–34)
The request of James and John (35–45)
The healing of blind Bartimaeus (46–52)

XI   JESUS IN JERUSALEM

The entry into the city (verses 1–11)
The unfruitful fig-tree (12–14)
The clearing of the Temple court (15–19)
The withered fig-tree (20–25)
The question of Jesus' authority (27–33)

XII   CONTROVERSY IN JERUSALEM

The parable of the vineyard (verses 1–12)
The question of tribute to the Romans (13–17)
A question about resurrection (18–27)
The question of the first commandment (28–34)
A question about David's son (35–37a)
Warnings against the scribes (37b–40)
The widow's mites (41–44)

Chapter

XIII APOCALYPTIC TEACHING

The coming destruction of the Temple (verses 1–4)
Signs of the end (5–13)
The horror to come (14–20)
Warnings against false Messiahs (21–23)
The appearance of the Son of Man (24–27)
The parable of the fig-tree (28–32)
The parable of the returning householder (33–37)

XIV THE TRIUMPH OF JESUS' ENEMIES

The conspiracy of the priests (verses 1–2)
The anointing of Jesus at Bethany (3–9)
The treachery of Judas (10–11)
The last supper (12–25)
Jesus and the disciples at the mount of Olives (26–42)
The arrest of Jesus (43–52)
Jesus before the high priest (53–65)
Denials by Peter (66–72)

XV THE TRIAL AND EXECUTION OF JESUS

The trial before Pilate (verses 1–20)
The crucifixion (21–32)
The death of Jesus (33–41)
The entombment of Jesus (42–47)

XVI AFTER THE CRUCIFIXION

The women's visit to the tomb (verses 1–8)
A summary of resurrection appearances (9–20)
Another summary

CHAPTER I

THE FIRST ACTIVITIES OF JESUS

THE PREACHING OF JOHN THE BAPTIST (verses 1–8)
(Matt. iii. 1–12. Luke iii. 1–20)

After giving quotations from the Old Testament, Mark describes the appearance of John. He called men to repent and be baptised and spoke of one who would succeed him and baptise people with the Spirit.

Mark opens his book with an abruptness which is typical of his writing. The first verse may have been intended as a title for the whole book, perhaps added after its completion, or it may be a 'heading' for the opening paragraph. In one sense the mission of John did constitute 'the beginning of the gospel', the inauguration of the Christian movement. The word 'gospel' here means a message of good news (see p. 11). The words 'Son of God', after 'Jesus Christ', are found in most manuscripts but are omitted in some Greek copies and early versions. The term probably means the same as 'Christ'. It is a designation which would be more easily understood by Mark's Gentile readers than the Jewish term 'Messiah'.

Mark states that the Old Testament quotations in verses 2–3 came from the prophet Isaiah. This is not strictly correct, as they are a combination of Exod. xxiii. 20 and Mal. iii. 1 (verse 2), to which is added Isa. xl. 3 (verse 3). Consequently later scribes altered the wording to read 'in the prophets', to correct Mark's mistake. None of these passages originally related to the messianic expectation or movement, although Mark makes them apply to the forerunner of the Messiah. Exod. xxiii. 20 is a promise to the Israelites that God's messenger or angel (or herald–N.E.B.) would go before them, as a guide and protector. The words in Mal. iii. 1 ('to prepare the way') are related to a threat of judgment on the prophet's own contemporaries. Isa. xl. 3 (verse 3) referred to the return of the Jews from Babylon, where they had been in exile; they were assured that God would lead them back across the Arabian desert. The parallelism of the Hebrew shows that the correct rendering is: 'Prepare in the wilderness the way of Yahweh; make straight in the desert a highway for our God.' Mark quotes from the Greek version of the Old Testament (the Septuagint, or LXX) and, applying the words to John, thinks of the 'desert' as the wilderness of Judea. This was the barren country west of the Dead Sea. The discovery of the Dead Sea scrolls in the caves and the unearthing of buildings at Qumran show that in the first century a monastic Jewish community lived there, which is generally identified with the Essenes. Some think that John had some contact with them, although it is unlikely that he was himself a member of the sect.

Baptism was known as a religious rite before this time. The word 'baptise' means literally 'dip', and in many religions initiates were bathed or sprinkled with water as a sign of purification. The Qumran sect frequently indulged in washings and baptisms. Among the Jews, proselytes (Gentiles who accepted the Jewish religion) were circumcised and baptised, to show that they had thrown off the evils of their past lives. The action of John was distinctive in that he baptised Jews. He said that they were thereby assured of remission or forgiveness of their sins, if they showed repentance (verse 4). Repentance meant a change of mind, not simply being sorry. But it was not so much an intellectual change as a moral one, a turning from the old way to a new life.

The description of John's clothing (verse 6) is taken from 2 Kings i. 8, an account of the prophet Elijah. His diet of 'locusts' may have been the insect, which can be cooked and eaten, or the locust-bean, the pods of the carob-tree. The 'honey' was the produce of the wild bees, which they stored in crevices in the rocks.

John stated that he was the forerunner of a mightier one (verse 7) but he did not specify this as the Messiah. According to Mal. iv. 5 and Jewish traditions, Elijah would come before the final 'day', and John may have been thinking of his successor as Elijah returned to earth. He said that he was not worthy to undertake the task of unloosening the thongs of that man's sandals. This was the task of a slave. A spiritual 'baptism' was also foreseen by John, to replace his water-baptism (verse 8). The Jews were familiar with the idea of God's holy Spirit. In the Old Testament it meant new life for a dead nation (Ezek. xxxvii. 14) and new power, and one of the signs of the 'last age' was to be the coming of the Spirit to men (Joel ii. 28f.).

THE BAPTISM AND TEMPTATION OF JESUS (verses 9–13)
(Matt. iii. 13–17; iv. 1–11. Luke iii. 21–22; iv. 1–13)

When Jesus was baptised, he experienced the presence of the Spirit and heard the voice of God. He then went into the wilderness for a period and faced temptations.

Mark brings Jesus on to the scene, as he had with John, without introduction to his readers; he naturally assumed they were familiar with the names. Nazareth (verse 9) is evidently thought of as Jesus' home town. It was about sixteen miles south-west of the lake of Galilee.

Mark describes the experience of Jesus himself, in symbolic language. He says 'the heavens opened', a 'voice' was heard and (later, verse 13) angels helped Jesus. These are Jewish ways of describing the presence of God. The words of the voice were evidently addressed to Jesus alone; the occasion would have no special significance for John or other people who may have been present. Mark also says that the Spirit came upon Jesus 'like a dove'. The phrase is metaphorical, not suggesting that an actual dove appeared. The dove symbolised gentleness (cf. Matt. x. 16). Mark may also have been thinking of the reference in Gen. i. 2 to the Spirit of God as 'moving upon' (or 'brooding upon') the water, in the creation story, which a first-century rabbi said was like the hovering of a dove. The early Hebrew idea of the Spirit was often that of a violent influence upon men. Mark speaks of a gentle and peaceful presence.

In the Old Testament days the Spirit came to men who were called to be prophets (e.g. Isa. lx. 1). So here Jesus received his call, which is expressed in words which recall two Old Testament passages (verse 11). Ps. ii. 7 reads: 'Thou art my son; this day I have become thy father.' This was addressed to a Jewish king who had so pleased God that he could call him his son. It was not originally messianic but was presumably taken by first-century Jews to refer to the Messiah. It was certainly so regarded later by the Christians. The rest of the statement, 'with thee I am well pleased' ('on thee my favour rests'–N.E.B.), is reminiscent of Isa. xlii. 1: 'my servant ... my chosen, in whom my soul delights'. This is a passage from one of the 'Servant-songs', in which an unknown prophet in the exile in Babylon wrote of a suffering servant of Yahweh. Mark thus relates that at his baptism Jesus received the Spirit of God and heard a call to be the Messiah and Servant.

Mark then says that the Spirit 'drove' Jesus into the wilderness (verse 12). This would be the wilderness of Judea, west of the Dead Sea, where John had been preaching. Mark says that he was 'tempted' (or, rather, 'tested') by Satan. This was a Hebrew word which originally meant an opponent or accuser of any kind. An adversary of the Hebrews from a foreign country was called a satan in the Old Testament. Later on the word was applied to one of the heavenly host before God (Job i. 6), who was allowed to act as 'counsel for the prosecution', to accuse good men (cf. Zech. iii. 1ff.). It was probably under Persian influence that the Jews extended the idea and came to think of a particular evil being who was the opponent of God. The Greek word 'devil' (which also meant slanderer) was sometimes used of him. By the first century Satan was regarded by the Jews as the head of a kingdom of evil (cf. Mark iii, 23–24).

A fuller account of the temptations which Jesus faced was included in the document Q, used by Matthew and Luke. Jesus was here probably considering the methods he was to adopt in his work, to make the kingdom of God a reality in the lives of men. The account from Q shows that he rejected the methods suggested by the current Jewish ideas of how the Messiah would work.

JESUS' FIRST PREACHING AND CALL OF DISCIPLES (verses 14–20)
(Matt. iv. 12–22. Luke iv. 14–15; v. 1–11)

Jesus began his public work in Galilee by proclaiming the kingdom of God. He called four fishermen at the lake to follow him.

Mark assumes that his readers are familiar with the fact of John's imprisonment (verse 14), which he relates later on (vi. 17). Perhaps he suggests that this was the reason for Jesus' return to Galilee and the beginning of his own work. He takes up the message of John, 'Repent', with a significant addition—'believe in the gospel'. This phrase here means the message preached by Jesus. It was 'good news about God', or 'good news from God'. The phrase 'The time is fulfilled' ('The time has come'–N.E.B.) means that the time of deliverance by God, waited for by Old Testament prophets and the Jews of his own time, had now arrived—yet in a different way from that of the popular expectation. The term 'kingdom of God' occurs fourteen times in Mark. It means the kingly rule or reign of God and was the theme of Jesus' teaching and parables. The proclamation here is that the kingdom 'is at hand' or 'is upon you'. It might mean 'The kingdom of God has arrived', showing that Jesus was proclaiming the presence of God's rule as a reality among men, rather than its near advent.

The sea of Galilee (verse 16) from which Jesus called his first followers is more correctly called a lake (modern Lake Tiberias). It is twelve miles from north to south and six miles at its extreme breadth. Fishing was one of the staple industries in the towns and villages on its shores. There had surely been some previous acquaintance with these men, or they would not have followed so readily at Jesus' command.

Jesus' First Preaching in Capernaum (verses 21–28)
(Matt. vii. 28–29. Luke iv. 31–37)

On the Sabbath Jesus spoke with authority in the synagogue at Capernaum and cured a frenzied man, to the astonishment of the people.

Capernaum was a town on the northern shore of the lake, west of the river Jordan. The ruins of the city of Tell Hum, which include a synagogue, have been excavated on the probable site, but they do not go back to the time of Jesus. Many of his early activities as recorded in Mark took place here and he seems to have made it his headquarters.

As loyal Jews, Jesus and his companions would attend the local synagogue on the Sabbath. The word Sabbath literally means 'rest' and it was the last day of the week, corresponding to our Saturday. In accordance with the law of the Old Testament, no work was permitted on that day, but it was a time for worship in the synagogue and for social intercourse. Mark tells later of occasions on which Jesus came into conflict with those who upheld the strict interpretation of this law. The word 'synagogue' is a Greek one meaning an assembly. Synagogues were probably started when the Jews were in exile in Babylon, in the sixth century B.C. Sacrificial worship was then no longer possible, as the Temple had been destroyed, but the Jews could not give up their worship, so they assembled for prayer and the reading of their scriptures and instruction in their religious duties. The practice of meeting in this way has been

continued up to the present time. In Jesus' time every
town or village had one or more synagogues, in Palestine and throughout the Roman world, wherever there
were Jews living.

The service in the synagogue was a simple one, consisting of the recitation of passages from the Old Testament, prayers, the chanting of psalms, two readings (one
from the Law and the other from the Prophets) and an
address. The synagogue was in the charge of elders—
leading men of the locality, who could invite a visitor or
member of the congregation to take part in the worship
by reading and speaking. Jesus was apparently already
known as a religious teacher and so was invited to give
the address.

The people in the congregation compared Jesus'
teaching, with its note of authority, with that of the
scribes (or doctors of the law–N.E.B.). These men were
originally the copyists of the manuscripts of the Old
Testament books; hence they became, through their
acquaintance with the text, the leading interpreters and
authorities on the Law. The remark of the people
suggests that the teaching which the scribes gave in the
synagogue tended to be second-hand, rather than having original authority such as Jesus showed, although
he had had no technical rabbinic training.

The service was apparently interrupted by the cry of
a man who had an 'unclean spirit' (verse 23). This
probably means that he was suffering from hysteria (as
we might put it) and there was thought to be within
him a demon which made him do 'unclean things'—
not necessarily repulsive actions but things which were
forbidden from the point of view of the Jewish Law. It
was generally thought in the ancient world that certain
disorders, particularly of the mind or nervous system,

were to be credited to demon-possession. The action of expelling a demon or spirit from the body of a man or animal was known as exorcism. This was practised by other people besides Jesus, although his success here, as well as his authoritative manner, further impressed the people of Capernaum (verse 27). The cry of the man (verse 24) is a Hebrew idiom which meant 'What have we in common?'—with the implication that the speaker did not want to have anything to do with the person he addressed. It might be translated: 'Why do you interfere with me?' The term with which the man addressed Jesus—'holy one of God'—is probably not a messianic title but indicates that he recognised something different or 'holy' about Jesus. People who are not in full possession of their normal faculties often do have such 'second sight'.

THE CURE OF PETER'S MOTHER-IN-LAW AND OTHERS (verses 29–34)
(Matt. viii. 14–17. Luke iv. 38–41)

After the synagogue service Jesus went to the house of Peter and Andrew where he cured Peter's wife's mother of fever. After sunset, people flocked around him to be cured.

The fact that Peter was married is confirmed by Paul (1 Cor. ix. 5); other apostles probably were also. His mother-in-law may have had malaria; fever occurred frequently in the low-lying districts around the lake. Capernaum was apparently the home town of Peter and Andrew. Mark then gives (verse 32) a generalised account of a typical scene of healing. The Sabbath ended at sunset and it would be against the Law for people to bring their sick folk before then. The demoniacs (sufferers whose state was considered to be due to demon-possession) are here distinguished from those who were merely ill (verse 34). Jesus usually enjoined silence on those whom he cured or on the spirits which he expelled.

The Greek word which is usually translated 'devils' (verse 34) is a different one from the word used to designate Satan or 'the devil'; it should be rendered 'demons'. There was considered to be only one devil but there were numerous demons, which were thought to people the world, finding a home in a human or animal body or living in desert or uncanny places or in the 'air' between earth and heaven.

A WITHDRAWAL OF JESUS (verses 35–39)
(Matt. iv. 23–25. Luke iv. 42–44)

Next day Jesus left Capernaum early, to pray. When the disciples followed him he said he had to go to other places to preach. He then went on a tour of Galilee.

The 'desert place' (verse 35) does not mean the wilderness but simply a lonely spot (as N.E.B.) outside the city. Some think that Jesus deliberately left Capernaum because he was in danger of being regarded and followed as a healer and wonder-worker. His reply to the remark of the disciples—'that is why I came out' (verse 38)—may refer simply to his departure from Capernaum. But Mark may have been thinking of Jesus' mission as a whole.

THE HEALING OF A LEPER (verses 40–45)
Matt. viii. 1–4. Luke v. 12–16)

A leper begged Jesus to make him clean. With emotion Jesus responded and told the leper to carry out the Jewish Law and to tell nobody of his cure.

No indication is given where this incident took place —presumably on Jesus' preaching tour of Galilee. Mark was simply relating typical stories of Jesus' activities at the beginning of his work and was not interested in questions of geographical location or chronological sequence. The term leprosy was often applied in the first century to various skin diseases, some of them of a temporary duration and a comparatively mild nature, not necessarily the terrible, repulsive disease we connect with the word leper. Such a skin disease made the sufferer 'unclean', from the religious point of view. He was forbidden to enter a house and had to warn people of his approach by crying 'Unclean, unclean!' (Lev. xiii. 45–46) By touching the man (verse 41) Jesus put himself 'outside the pale' and made himself also, for the time, ceremonially unclean. The leper's cry (verse 40) could, however, mean 'You can pronounce me clean', in which case he was asking Jesus to act the part of a priest, whose duty it was to pronounce a man clean if he thought he was cured.

Instead of the Greek word for 'being moved with compassion' (verse 41), some manuscripts have a word meaning 'being angry' (N.E.B.: 'in warm indignation'). If this is what Mark wrote, he may have meant that Jesus was angry at the leper's approach, since he was supposed to keep away from other people. Or Jesus may have been angry at the implication in the man's request—'if you will'—that he was not willing to help him. Mark uses other strong words in verse 43, suggesting that he turned the man out; perhaps the incident happened in a house, where the man had no right to be. These vivid features in the story suggest the reminiscences of an eyewitness, who remembered the vigour and sternness of Jesus' treatment of the man. Jesus then told the man to observe the legal regulations; he was not allowed to mix with his fellows until he had reported to a priest, offered a sacrifice and received a statement that he really was cured (Lev. xiii. 39ff.). Jesus also told the man to say nothing about his cure; it was generally thought that he wished to avoid the kind of popularity and attention which he actually received when the man disobeyed him (verse 45).

The account of Jesus' work in Galilee is continued in Mark iii. 7–12. The writer now interposes a series of incidents illustrating the opposition with which Jesus met.

CHAPTER II

OPPOSITION TO JESUS

AFTER the introductory account of Jesus' first preaching and healing, in chapter i, Mark gives a series of 'conflict-stories' to show how Jesus met various opponents (ii. 1 to iii. 6). These deal with complaints made on account of his authority, his fellowship with sinners, his neglect of fasting and his treatment of the Sabbath.

THE HEALING OF A PARALYSED MAN (verses 1–12)
(Matt. ix. 1–8. Luke v. 17–26)

A paralytic was brought by his friends before Jesus, who told him that his sins were forgiven. In response to criticism from the scribes, he told the man to walk.

It is not clear in whose 'house' (verse 1) this event took place; the Greek phrase could simply mean 'at home' (as in N.E.B.). It might have been Peter's house in Capernaum. When Mark says that the men 'opened up the roof' (literally: 'dug through the roof') (verse 4), he is thinking of a simple Palestinian house with a flat roof of hard earth over beams and matting, which could be reached from the outside. The bed (R.V.) or stretcher (N.E.B.) on which the man was lying was simply a pallet or mat and could easily be carried. The writers of Matthew and Luke avoided the word, probably because they thought it too colloquial.

The statement that Jesus 'saw their faith' (verse 5)

suggests at first sight, if the phrase refers merely to the four friends, that a man might be saved or cured through the faith of someone else. But the remark probably includes the man himself, for he was surely willing for his friends to bring him before Jesus with the belief that he could be cured. In objecting to the statement of Jesus to the man about the forgiveness of his sins, the scribes missed the point. Jesus did not say that he himself forgave the man's sins but declared that they had been forgiven, by God. The scribes (see p. 56 for an account of these) thought that Jesus had committed blasphemy. This word was used in classical Greek to describe slander against men or the gods. Among the Jews blasphemy consisted in the improper use of the name of God. It was evidently applied, in a more loose way, to religious offences such as taking too much upon oneself or saying things which would detract from the majesty or honour of God. The scribes were here acting as the upholders of orthodox Jewish religion.

Jesus recognised intuitively (verse 8) the comments of the objectors. Mark thought of him as exercising the insight into men's characters which was a feature of the prophetic gift. The attitude and countenances of his critics, as well as their muttered comments, would betray their thoughts.

Among ancient peoples (not only among the Jews) illness was often thought of as a punishment by God for a man's evil deeds. Jesus never endorsed this view; he never said that all sickness was the result of sin. This man's physical state, however, may have been due to the kind of life he had lived, so Jesus first set his mind at rest. In reply to the criticisms of the onlookers he pointed out that it was obviously easier to tell a man that his sins had been forgiven than to tell him to walk (verse 9). So he now proceeded to do the more difficult thing, apparently suggesting that the scribes ought to accept his earlier words, that the man had been forgiven, if they saw him cured.

The connection may not seem very clear and it has been suggested that two stories have been combined in this narrative. One was a straightforward healing-story, in which stress was laid on the efforts of the man and his friends. The account ran: 'When Jesus saw their faith, he said to the paralytic: I say to you, Take up your pallet and go home.' In another story Jesus told a sufferer that his sins were forgiven and the intervening section (verses 5b–10) is part of this narrative.

The term Son of Man occurs here (verse 10) for the first time in Mark. In the Semitic idiom the phrase means simply 'a man' and it is used in this way in the Old Testament (e.g. Ps. viii. 4, where 'man' and 'son of man' are parallel). Some have thought that here it has this meaning, that 'man on earth' has the right to pronounce the forgiveness awarded by God. But such an idea seems to have no point here and it was quite alien to Jewish thought. Jesus may have meant himself, using the term Son of Man as equivalent to the Messiah; but it is strange to find him making a claim so early in his ministry. The phrase is not used in Mark (apart from here and ii. 28) until Peter acknowledged Jesus as Messiah, at Caesarea Philippi (viii. 27ff.); and Jesus never publicly claimed to be Messiah until he was challenged by the high priest at his trial (xiv. 62). This leads to the question: were these words spoken by Jesus? Verse 10 is not really part of the narrative but is a parenthesis. Without this verse the account reads more smoothly. Many have hence concluded that this is an addition to the story by a narrator—perhaps by Mark himself or by someone when the story was told orally. He assured his hearers that Jesus cured the man 'that *you* may know the Son of Man [that is, Jesus himself] has authority to forgive sins'.

THE CALL OF LEVI AND ITS SEQUEL (verses 13–17)
(Matt. ix. 9–13. Luke v. 27–32)

Jesus called a tax-collector to follow him. At a meal afterwards he was criticised for mixing with sinful people, but he justified his conduct.

Levi had probably heard Jesus preach, as he followed him so readily. He may have been a tax-gatherer in the service of Herod Antipas, collecting dues from people entering Galilee from the territory of Herod Philip, on the road which ran from Capernaum to Damascus. The name of Matthew is substituted for that of Levi in the parallel passage (based on Mark) in Matt. ix. 9 and in the list of the twelve apostles in that Gospel Matthew is called 'the tax-collector'. But Mark gives no indication that Levi and Matthew were the same man and suggests no change of name on the part of Levi. He does include James the son of Alphaeus in the list of apostles, and it is possible that he and Levi were the same.

Mark does not make it clear in whose house (verse 15) Jesus was having a meal. Possibly it was Levi's or the house which Jesus himself was occupying. The tax-gatherers mentioned here were minor officials. They were in the pay of the *publicani*—men who were in charge of the general collection of revenue, after having obtained that privilege from the Roman State. They collected money which eventually went into the pockets of the Roman overlords, after a profit had been made by a number of people through whose hands it passed. So the Jews hated all grades of tax-collectors, not only because they worked for a foreign power but also because they were non-religious folk, mixing and having business dealings with Gentiles. The 'sinners' with whom they are here associated (verse 16) were not necessarily people who lived very bad lives but people who were not scrupulously religious and did not obey all the Jewish Law. In reply to the criticism of his conduct Jesus quotes a popular proverb about a doctor (verse 17) and speaks of 'inviting' sinners, not righteous people. The terms reflect ironically those no doubt used by his 'righteous' critics.

Pharisees are mentioned here for the first time (verse 16). The name is generally taken to mean 'the separated (party)'. It may have been used originally to stress the separation of the Jews from other nations and applied later to the distinction between the Pharisees and ordinary Jewish people. The title may also have been used to stress that they were 'separate' from all that was wrong in the sight of God. This religious sect or society arose in the second century B.C. When the country was in danger of being infected with pagan ideas and practices, they led a movement back to the Jewish Bible, calling the people to a study of the Law and its application to everyday life. The Pharisees were mostly laymen, with rules for the admission of new members. Some were businessmen, shopkeepers, artisans, teachers. They tended to regard with scorn the people who did not come up to their own rigorous standards.

A Question About Fasting (verses 18–22)
(Matt. ix. 14–17. Luke v. 33–39)

Jesus was asked why his disciples neglected fasting. His reply showed the difference between strict legal religion and his own teaching.

Mark does not say who were the people who here questioned Jesus. Strict Jews used to fast on Mondays and Thursdays. The disciples of John the baptist may have been following the Jewish practice. It has been suggested that they were fasting in mourning for their master, after his death, in which case this incident happened later and has been placed here by Mark for convenience, as part of his collection of conflict-stories. This would certainly give more point to the remarks in verses 19–20 about the presence or absence of the bridegroom, indicating that Jesus was still with his disciples, whereas John had been taken away from them.

The phrase 'disciples of the Pharisees' (verse 19) is a strange one, for the Pharisees were not specifically teachers who had disciples. It may be a general term for those who adopted Pharisaic practices.

In his reply Jesus pointed out that his company was more like a wedding party than a mourning party. But among the Jews the Messiah was often spoken of as a bridegroom and the kingdom as a wedding feast, so a deeper hint of Jesus' position may be implied here. The 'sons of the bridechamber' (R.V.) or the 'bridegroom's friends' (N.E.B.) were the groomsmen or the wedding guests (R.S.V.). The statement in verse 20 that the bridegroom would be 'snatched away' (as the Greek verb literally means) would be meaningless to Jesus' immediate hearers in this context. If the statement was uttered by Jesus, it was perhaps on a later occasion, as a warning to his disciples. It is more probable, however, that it is a later addition by a Christian teacher who wanted to round off Jesus' statement in verse 19 by bringing in a reference to his death.

The two statements about the piece of cloth and the wineskins (verses 20–21) are illustrations of the impossibility of combining old and new. They were probably uttered on a different occasion. They mean that the traditional religion of Judaism cannot be 'patched up' to make Jesus' teaching fit it, and that it is impossible to contain the new teaching in the old receptacles. The 'cloth' with which the garment is patched is new, so when it gets wet it shrinks and tears away from the material of the garment. The wineskins were not 'bottles' but were of leather. New wine put into them would ferment and new skins would 'give'; but old skins, already stretched, would not 'give' but would burst.

AN INCIDENT IN THE CORNFIELDS (verses 23–28)
   (Matt. xii. 1–8. Luke vi. 1–5)

Jesus was attacked because his disciples were 'working' by plucking ears of corn on the Sabbath. In reply he referred to a time when David broke the Law and enunciated a principle about the use of the Sabbath for man.

This is the first of the controversies about Jesus' attitude towards the Sabbath. The ripe corn suggests that the time was between April and June. It was considered by strict Jews that to pluck the ears of corn and rub them with the hands was equivalent to reaping and threshing and thus constituted work, which was forbidden on the Sabbath.

Jesus' reply to the complaint was threefold. He first gave a reference to Hebrew history. When David was fleeing from king Saul he came with his men to the tabernacle at Nob and asked the priest for some food. The priest had none except the shewbread ('bread of the presence')—twelve newly-baked loaves which were placed on a table every Sabbath and eaten later by the priests. The name of the priest in this case was not Abiathar, as Mark says, but Ahimelech (1 Sam. xxi. 1–6). Either Jesus or Mark made a mistake. The case of David was not a perfect parallel, for the incident did not take place on a Sabbath, but Jesus was pointing out that even the Law must be subservient to human needs.

Jesus then enunciated two principles about the use of the Sabbath. The Jewish rabbis would have agreed with the first, that the Sabbath was instituted for the use and delight of men (verse 27). But the second (verse 28) is a difficulty, for the term Son of Man is here used early in Mark (as in ii. 10) and in a way without parallel in the Gospel. There are various views about the meaning here:

(i) That the phrase means simply 'man'. This follows from verse 27—as the Sabbath was made for man, so he has command over the Sabbath. But the Jews held (and Jesus would hold) that God was lord of the Sabbath, not man.

(ii) That it refers to Jesus himself, as Messiah. But lordship of the Sabbath was not considered a messianic function and Jesus makes no similar claim elsewhere.

(iii) That it means Jesus' disciples, as representative of the messianic community, as the complaint had been made against them. An objection to the last two suggestions is that such a statement by Jesus would be quite enigmatic to his hearers.

(iv) That the verse is an addition, a comment by a narrator or by Mark himself. He pointed out Jesus' authority to decide about the Sabbath. This would be of interest to Gentile Christians, as some Jewish believers would try to enforce on them the strict observance of the Sabbath. So the narrator pointed out that Jesus and his followers were above the mere rules of Sabbath-keeping.

CHAPTER III

FURTHER CAUSES OF OPPOSITION
AND MISUNDERSTANDING

THE CURE OF A MAN'S WITHERED HAND (verses 1–6)
(Matt. xii. 9–14. Luke vi. 6–11)

Faced with a sick man in the synagogue, Jesus challenged his opponents about the right to do good on the Sabbath. His attitude and his cure of the man led to a plot against him.

This is the last of the conflict-stories which began at ii. 1, although further on Mark gives some more cases of misunderstanding. Mark does not say who 'they' were who watched Jesus (verse 2). He may indicate simply curiosity on the part of the synagogue congregation, but the phrase suggests prior suspicion of Jesus or even that the man had been deliberately planted there with a view to trapping Jesus.

The man probably suffered from a local paralysis. The Jewish Law permitted medical aid to be given on a Sabbath only if life was in danger. Jesus' question (verse 4) put his opponents in a quandary; it was obviously not right to do evil on the Sabbath, but to agree that it was better to do good was to give Jesus permission to heal the man. The point of the second part of his question is that for Semites healing was equivalent to making alive, saving a life. Hence Jesus suggested that to leave the man in his present state would be equivalent to taking his life. Some have thought that Jesus was making a covert reference to the intention of his enemies to put *him* to death but the incident seems placed too early for this.

Jesus gave two commands to the man—to stand out (so that all might see him) and to stretch out his arm. In many instances Jesus asked a patient to do something by his own efforts (cf. ii. 11). It suggests he wanted the co-operation of the sufferer himself, in order to effect a cure.

The Herodians (verse 6) were politically-minded Jews who supported the Herod family. Perhaps they hoped for the restoration of a national kingdom such as there had been under Herod the Great. They are mentioned in the Gospels only here and in Mark xii. 13, where also they joined forces with the Pharisees, to ask Jesus a question about payment of taxes to the Romans. The Pharisees disregarded politics and it is strange to find the two parties allied. It is possible that Mark has placed this union of their forces too early, anticipating here what happened when Jesus was in Jerusalem. He inserts this final sentence to sum up the opposition to Jesus in Galilee and its ultimate result.

TEACHING BY THE LAKE (verses 7–12)
    (Matt. xii. 15–21. Luke vi. 17–19)

Jesus was followed by large numbers of people, whom he taught and healed. Demoniacs acknowledged him.

This is a summary paragraph composed by Mark. The provision of a boat (verse 9) is mentioned in order to prepare for its use in iv. 1. The districts named in verse 8 constituted the different parts of Palestine— Galilee in the north, Judea in the south, with the capital Jerusalem. Idumea was the Old Testament Edom; it had been conquered by the Jews about 128 B.C. and was now considered Jewish territory. The district 'beyond Jordan' (Transjordan–N.E.B.) was Perea, east of the Jordan and the Dead Sea. Tyre and Sidon were the chief ports of Phoenicia, on the north-west coast. Mark has already mentioned the recognition of Jesus by demons (i. 24; i. 34). Now he states that they called Jesus Son of God, which meant Messiah.

The Choice of Twelve Disciples (verses 13–19) (Matt. x. 1–4. Luke vi. 12–16)

From his company of followers Jesus chose twelve men.

Two purposes are noted for Jesus' choice of an inner circle—for fellowship with him and for practical work in preaching. It was a usual practice with religious teachers in the East to gather a band of special followers. The word 'disciple' means a pupil or follower, a man in training. Twelve were chosen by Jesus perhaps because this was a convenient number for such a fellowship and also because there were originally twelve tribes of the Hebrews. Jesus' company was thought of as representing the true Israel. The men are generally referred to as the twelve apostles, but they are called this in Mark only at vi. 30. The word 'apostle' is derived from a Greek verb meaning 'send out' and the word was in general use in the first century to denote a messenger or envoy. An apostle is thus a special kind of disciple, one who not only follows his master but goes forth in his name. Nothing further is known about many of the men who are named here, apart from the leading members of the band.

The name Peter, which was given to Simon (verse 16), means a rock (Greek *Petros*; the Aramaic *Kephas* has the same meaning). It may have been given as an indication of the possibilities in Simon's character, for he is certainly not rock-like as portrayed in the Gospels. Boanerges, the name given to the sons of Zebedee, is neither Hebrew nor Aramaic nor Greek and we cannot tell why Mark says it meant 'sons of thunder'. (In the Semitic idiom the 'son of' a person or a quality was one who shared his or its characteristics.) The name may have reference to some physical peculiarity such as deep voices or to their personal character as being rather stormy. The other Simon (a very common Jewish name) has the title Cananaean attached to him. This has nothing to do with Cana or Canaan but is an Aramaic word meaning 'zealous'. The designation may mean simply that he was a zealous Jew, but it is generally considered that he was a member of the Zealots or that he shared their views. Luke (vi. 15) takes it to mean this. The Zealots were fanatical nationalists, dedicated to the overthrow of the power of Rome, advocating this on religious as well as political grounds. The meaning of the name Iscariot is uncertain. Some think that it means 'a man (*ish*) of Kerioth'—a town in the south of Judea. In this case Judas might have been the only non-Galilean among the twelve. Another suggestion is that it represents the Latin *sicarius*—a 'dagger-man', belonging to the Zealots. The name may, however, be simply a nickname, perhaps given to him in contempt, the origin of which is unknown.

THE ANXIETY OF JESUS' FRIENDS (verses 20–21)

Jesus was so taken up with his work that those who were near him thought he was mad.

The remark that Jesus was thought to be 'out of his

mind' or 'beside himself' may go back to the view of a prophet which is sometimes found in the Old Testament. When he grew excited about his message, he was called a 'mad fellow'. It is not certain who the people were who thought this about Jesus. The Greek phrase is literally 'those about him', translated as 'his friends' (R.V.) or 'his family' (N.E.B.). Mark probably means his mother and brothers and sisters, in which case this narrative is continued in verses 31–35, where these members of his family approach him. Otherwise this short section seems pointless, without any sequel. Mark is fond of inserting a narrative (verses 22–30) into his account of another episode. Matthew and Luke do not reproduce these two verses.

THE ACCUSATION OF JESUS' ENEMIES (verses 22–30)
(Matt. xii. 22–37. Luke xi. 14–23)

Scribes from Jerusalem said that Jesus used the power of the prince of demons in his exorcisms. He showed the absurdity of the charge and warned people against the seriousness of such an offence.

Jesus' opponents could not deny his power in practising exorcism but they attributed his success to his being in league with Beelzebub. The Greek word is Beelzebul. Beelzebub was the name of a god of the Philistines in the Old Testament, which meant 'lord of flies'. This may have been a contemptuous alteration by the Hebrews of the name Beelzebul, which meant 'lord of the lofty dwelling', i.e. heaven, or the abode of the gods. In New Testament times the name was used for the 'prince of demons', who was thought of as having his realm in opposition to the kingdom of God. By another slight alteration of the word, the name could also mean 'lord of enmity', which would correspond to the terms used for the devil—Hebrew *satan* or adversary and Greek *diabolos* or slanderer.

Jesus' reply to the accusation was threefold: (i) To say that Beelzebub drives out his own demons is absurd. This would mean civil war (verses 24–26). (ii) Beelzebub is strong in his own house until someone binds him and plunders his goods (verse 27). Jesus suggests that by his own work Beelzebub is being 'bound'. Hence his power must be greater than that of Beelzebub and must have another source. (iii) Such an accusation means blasphemy against the Spirit of God (verses 28–29). This 'blasphemy' is the tendency to ascribe to an evil power that which is plainly due to a power which is good and holy—the Spirit of God. This failure to differentiate between good and evil renders a man incapable of moral discrimination and exhibits a warped sense of judgment. It is an 'eternal' sin, the adjective expressing the quality of the offence, not its duration. Such a man is beyond forgiveness, at least while he remains in that condition.

JESUS' TRUE FAMILY (verses 31–35)
    (Matt. xii. 46–50. Luke viii. 19–21)

Jesus was told of the anxiety of his relatives. He pointed out a wider relationship than the earthly one.

This incident is often regarded as the sequel to verses 20–21. No mention is made here of Jesus' father, Joseph; he was probably dead by this time. His brothers and sisters are mentioned also at Nazareth in vi. 3. Some have suggested that these were the children of Joseph by a former wife, before he married Mary. But there is no evidence for such a marriage, in the New Testament or elsewhere. In the fourth century Jerome suggested that 'brothers' meant 'cousins'. But a different Greek word was used for cousins, which Mark would surely have used if he meant this. And why should cousins accompany Mary to come and see Jesus? The natural conclusion is that Jesus' brothers and sisters were the children of Mary and Joseph, born after Jesus, who is indeed called Mary's 'first' son in Luke ii. 7.

In his reply (verses 34–35) Jesus did not repudiate the family relationship, but said that his true family was a wider one. He frequently emphasised the importance of doing the will of God.

CHAPTER IV

TEACHING BY PARABLES

THE PARABLE OF THE SOWER (verses 1–9)
(Matt. xiii. 1–9. Luke viii. 4–8)

Jesus taught by the lakeside and told a parable about a sower and the results of his sowing.

After relating instances of opposition to Jesus and his work, Mark turns to his teaching and gives examples of his parables. The matter here was probably already collected together; it is unlikely that all this teaching was given on one occasion or in the order presented here. Mark gives his own setting for this material, picturing Jesus as sitting in a boat and using that as a platform; the reference to a boat in iii. 9 prepared for this, although much is stated to have happened in the meantime.

The word parable is derived from two Greek words, *para* (by the side of) and *ballo* (I put). A parable is thus a comparison between two things which are placed alongside. In the Gospels a parable is generally a description or story in which the kingdom of God or some principle of his rule is compared with something in the life of men. Most of the Markan parables are of this type. It is generally considered today that each of the parables told by Jesus had one main point which he desired to convey. This must be sought first in the immediate situation in which he spoke. The intention of a parable was to stir the minds of the hearers or the readers, to awaken them to the recognition of a particular situation and to challenge them to action. Parables must not be treated as allegories (in which each item is significant and corresponds to something else) or as fables (which are imaginary stories told to point a moral). To treat them as such is to make them lose their reality and vitality and to rob them of their significance and relevance to Jesus' original hearers.

The parable of the sower starts with a description which would be familiar to Galileans. The man would be sowing 'broadcast', throwing the seed to right and left as he walked down the field. The reception given to the seed in different types of soil is described. The 'wayside' or footpath (verse 4) would be the path running across the field. The rocky ground (verse 5) indicates the rock under a thin layer of soil. The thorns or thistles (verse 7) are roots left in the soil when weeding was done. They creep up and choke the growing wheat. The emphasis in the parable appears to be on the remarkable results from the seed which fell on good earth (verse 8). The parable is thus an encouragement to the disciples in their work and a reflection of the success Jesus had had up to that time.

THE MEANING OF THE PARABLE (verses 10-20)
(Matt. xiii. 10-23. Luke viii. 9-15)

Jesus was asked by the disciples about the meaning of parables. He answered them by a quotation from Isaiah and an explanation of the parable of the sower.

A short conversation (verses 10-12) about the meaning of parables in general is inserted, before an interpretation is given of the parable of the sower. This is said to have occurred when Jesus was 'alone' with the twelve whom he had chosen, yet others were present—apparently interested hearers or disciples. The scene at the beginning of the chapter seems to have been forgotten. Jesus' reply (verse 11) appears to suggest two classes of people, the disciples whom he was addressing and people 'outside'. The former understand 'the mystery of the kingdom' but parables are told in order that the latter class shall not see, hear or understand. This is backed up by a quotation from Isa. vi. 9f. All this seems to suggest that Jesus told parables in order to obscure his meaning rather than to illuminate it.

This is plainly counter to the teaching and intention of Jesus, who surely wanted to help men to understand and sought to proclaim the truth, not to hide it. The quotation from Isaiah, however, which is part of the account of his call to be a prophet, describes the *result* of his preaching: men would become more dull of understanding through not heeding his message. He could probably see this issue from the beginning of his work. This is reproduced in Mark, with the introductory word translated 'so that' or 'in order that', as if it described the intention and purpose of Jesus' work. But the Semitic mind often did not make a clear distinction between purpose and result. Jesus may have felt that in this respect his work was to be like that of Isaiah. Even though he tried to make the truth plain by using parables, men would not understand. It has been suggested that the Greek word which implies purpose is a translation of an Aramaic word meaning 'who'. The quotation then describes the people who 'are without'— they are the people who 'see but do not perceive . . .' (N.E.B.: look and look but see nothing).

It is quite probable that the quotation from Isaiah

was not spoken by Jesus on this occasion. He may have remarked on the difference between the disciples who understood the 'mystery of the kingdom' and those who did not, and Mark (or some early Christian preacher) may have felt that the way in which Jesus' words were received was a fulfilment of prophecy and parallel with the experience of Isaiah and so provided here an Old Testament quotation to illustrate this.

The word 'mystery' occurs in the Gospels only here (verse 11) and in the parallels in Matthew and Luke. In Paul's writings it is found when he speaks of the 'mystery' of God's purpose for men; he means a secret which is now revealed. There are various views as to what is the 'mystery of the kingdom' which is here referred to:

(i) Mark may have been thinking in terms of the 'mystery religions' of the first-century pagan world. Those who joined such cults were made aware of revelations from a god which were kept secret from ordinary men. In this case Christianity would be regarded as a 'mystery' into which men were initiated. It is very unlikely that this was the meaning which Jesus intended.

(ii) The mystery may be the interpretation of parables, which was granted to a few, such as the explanation of the parable of the sower which follows. But most of the parables do not seem to need any such 'secret' explanation.

(iii) It may refer to Jesus' method of establishing the kingdom of God—not by force but by persuasion and service. Jesus' circle of disciples realised this, in contrast to such men as the Zealots.

(iv) The secret may be the fact that the kingdom has arrived, in the teaching and work of Jesus himself,

announced in his first proclamation (Mark i. 15). Only
a few people realised this.

A somewhat elaborate explanation of the parable of
the sower follows (verses 17–20). There are several
difficulties in this. In the parable the emphasis is on the
different kinds of soil on which the seed falls; the seeds
are not differentiated. But in the interpretation the seeds
are of different kinds (e.g. verse 15 is literally 'the
[seeds] sown along the footpath are people in whom the
word is sown'; verse 18: 'the seeds sown among thorns
are those who hear the word ...') and the general
impression is very confusing. This makes the parable
into an allegory. The birds are said to stand for Satan,
the thorns stand for the cares of the world, etc. (verses
15, 19). Such an elaborate scheme is not inherent in the
parable itself. The main point also is changed. In the
parable the emphasis is on the good results, in spite of
some disappointment. In the interpretation the emphasis is on the seeds which fail to produce fruit.

The interpretation indeed, instead of illuminating the
parable, makes it more difficult to understand. It is
generally thought today that it did not come from
Jesus' teaching but was an explanation current in the
time of Mark and represents the exegesis of a Christian
teacher.

PARABOLIC SAYINGS (verses 21–25)
    (Luke viii. 16–18)
    A number of sayings are grouped together, with little
if any connection between them—about the function of
a lamp (verse 21), about proclaiming a secret (verse 22),
about judging (verse 24) and about increase in possessions (verse 25). There were parallels to these in the
document Q, for they are found also in Matthew and

Luke in places where these writers are not using Markan material. Mark placed them here perhaps because he thought they had a bearing on the 'mystery' attached to the teaching by parables.

The sayings in verses 21–22 mean that the function of a lamp is not to be hidden but to shed light. So the truth which Jesus proclaimed, although for a time it seemed to be concealed from the crowds, would ultimately be revealed. The saying in verse 24 means: Take care what you listen to and do not judge people harshly. The saying in verse 25 expresses the truth that the person who possesses something seems to be often the one who gains even more. This does not relate here to material possessions but to spiritual or mental ones. It is a common experience that if a person makes use of his capabilities or gifts he finds that these increase; if he neglects them he eventually ceases to have them at all.

THE PARABLE OF THE SEED GROWING (verses 26–29)

This is the only parable which is peculiar to Mark. The other Synoptic writers thought perhaps that it was too much like the parable of the mustard seed or they did not like the statement that the earth produced fruit 'by itself' (the Greek word is the one from which we derive 'automatically'); this may seem to rule out the activity of God.

The parable is sometimes taken as being eschatological in character, the climax relating to the final judgment of men, which would be carried out by God. This was a common thought among the Jews of Jesus' time. The harvest was a metaphor for the judgment; the words here about the sickle are indeed a quotation from Joel iii. 13. The parable would thus mean that the kingdom of God grows unseen among men, until it reaches its consummation at the final day. C. H. Dodd, however, holds that the parable related to developments in Jesus' own work. He was proclaiming that the time of harvest had now arrived. It may be that the parable represents Jesus' answer to an attempt to link his preaching of the presence of the kingdom with the movement of the Zealots—fanatical nationalists who thought that they could bring in God's kingdom by force and political action. Jesus showed that God's rule could not be hastened by such methods. It was growing unseen among men.

The Parable of the Mustard Seed (verses 30–32)
(Matt. xiii. 31–32. Luke xiii. 18–19)

This parable also occurred in the document Q. It is probable that there was a Jewish proverbial saying, 'small as a grain of mustard seed'. In the East the plant grows to a height of eight feet and birds can take shelter from the heat of the sun under its leaves. A contrast is pointed out between the small seed and the big plant; so the kingdom of God starts in a small way but becomes something mighty.

In the Old Testament a tree was sometimes used as a symbol for a great empire, giving protection to subject peoples, as birds nest in a tree. So Jesus may have been suggesting here a universal kingdom, not confined to the Jews, although we must not allegorise every detail in this or any parable. Jesus may have had in mind his own welcome to outcasts and sinners, to whom he was extending the blessings of God's rule, a practice to which his critics objected. This would accord with Dodd's view that here there is the same emphasis as in the previous parable—the plant had grown, the kingdom had arrived and men were flowing into it.

The Use of Parables (verses 33–34)
(Matt. xiii. 34–35)

This is Mark's final comment on this collection of the sayings of Jesus. He again employs the view he has mentioned already (iv. 10, 13ff.)—that Jesus gave a private interpretation to his disciples of parables which to those outside were only riddles.

A Storm on the Lake (verses 35–41)
(Matt. viii. 23–27. Luke viii. 22–25)

A storm suddenly arose while Jesus and his disciples were crossing to the eastern side of the lake of Galilee. In their fear they awoke him but he gave words of command and the storm subsided.

After giving instances of the conflict between Jesus and the religious authorities (ii–iii) and examples of his parabolic teaching (iv. 1–34), Mark starts a new section, turning to the works of Jesus and giving an account of various 'miracles' (iv. 35–41; v; vi).

Sudden storms of wind are still common on the lake of Galilee, owing to its situation. The lake is 700 feet below sea-level and the air generally still and heavy. Cold winds rush down the valleys between the hills and through the ravines around the lake and the waters are violently stirred. These storms cease as suddenly as they begin and all is soon calm again.

Mark's account of the incident is particularly vivid, as he describes the swamping of the boat, Jesus asleep on the cushion and the rebuke that the disciples directed towards Jesus, suggesting that he had no concern for their perilous situation (verse 38). (This was changed by Luke and Matthew to a mere cry for help.) His words

translated 'Be still!' (verse 39) are literally 'Be muzzled'
—the same terms as those addressed to the possessed
man in the Capernaum synagogue (i. 25), as if there was
a demon in the storm. The narrator of the story evidently believed that by his command Jesus had stilled
the elements; the disciples themselves drew this inference
(verse 41). We have, however, no other evidence that
Jesus exercised control over the weather or the forces of
nature. Some consider that, even if he had such power,
he would not have been likely to make use of it. The
disciples had later on to face far worse situations than a
storm in Galilee and the tempests of life were not stilled
for their benefit. Perhaps the words of command—'Be
quiet!'—were addressed to the disciples, who were 'such
cowards' (verse 40–N.E.B.), and his words were misunderstood. He could see that the storm was only
temporary and himself exhibited the faith or confidence
that they lacked. The sudden cessation of the storm gave
the impression that Jesus had been responsible for this
and so the story was told as a 'nature miracle'. Some
commentators consider that it is impossible to reconstruct what actually happened and that the story was
an illustration of the fears of disciples in the storms of
life and the peace that comes from trusting in the power
of Jesus.

CHAPTER V

JESUS' WORKS OF POWER

THE CURE OF A DEMONIAC (verses 1–20)
(Matt. viii. 28–34. Luke viii. 26–39)

On the eastern shore of the lake Jesus met a madman living among tombs. After a conversation with the man, Jesus expelled the demons within him and a herd of pigs rushed to their destruction in the lake.

It had been evening when Jesus and the disciples had set out to cross the lake of Galilee (iv. 35), so this incident probably did not take place immediately on their landing from the boat. It may belong to another occasion. The name given to the district here is uncertain. Mark has Gerasenes (in the most trustworthy manuscripts). Matthew has Gadarenes; there was a town called Gadara about six miles away. The tombs among which the man lived (verse 3) would be caves on the hillside where the dead were buried. Such places would be shunned by everybody, for it was considered defilement to touch or enter a tomb. So the man would be safe from molestation there, after he had broken away from the people's attempts to restrain him (verse 4).

This story is one of the most vividly told in Mark. He gives a graphic description of the terrors of madness and the strength of the man and also reproduces first-century ideas about his condition. Such men were thought to be possessed by demons. These spirits had to find a home somewhere; if they could not inhabit a human body they took possession of an animal. Hence they asked to be allowed to go into the herd of pigs (verse 12). It was the practice among exorcists to demand the name of the spirit within a man; by this means they thought they would obtain power over it. Jesus asked the man his name (verse 9); he may have been following the usual method of the time or he may have been seeking to call the man to a sense of his own personality, as separate from the demons which were in him. The man's unexpected reply—'*My* name is Legion, for *we* are many'— well expresses the confusion in his own mind. The word 'legion' was a Latin term which meant a regiment of the Roman army—normally about 6000 men—but this was probably not meant literally here.

The man addressed Jesus as 'Son of the Most High God' (verse 7). This may have been a pagan way of speaking of the God of Israel and the man may have been a Gentile. This part of Palestine was inhabited mostly by Gentiles and the fact that pigs were kept in the locality shows that there were at least some Gentiles in the neighbourhood. The man resented the presence of Jesus, using the same language—'Why do you interfere with me?'—as the possessed people at Capernaum (i. 24; iii. 11).

Mark does not say that Jesus ordered the demons to go into the pigs, after leaving the man, but only that he agreed to their request (verse 13). Many have wondered if Jesus would have consented to the destruction of animals even as a demonstration that the man had been completely cured. It would seem to make him callous towards the animal world, whereas he elsewhere spoke feelingly of the loss of one sparrow. This view also involves accepting belief in demon-possession and first-century ideas about the supernatural world. It is more probable that the flight of the pigs was due to a paroxysm of the man or to his shouting, which drove them headlong in fear; the pigs may have been neglected by the herdsmen in their curiosity to overhear the conversation between Jesus and the man. The panic and destruction of the swine were naturally taken by the onlookers as evidence that the demons had been transferred from the man to the animals and this explanation became embedded in the story.

The people asked Jesus to leave the district (verse 17), apparently because his presence was considered too dangerous. The man was told to let others know what the Lord (meaning of course God) had done for him (verse 19); this was not Jesus' usual policy, for he had enjoined silence on those whom he cured (i. 44; iii. 12). Perhaps he altered his instructions here because he was not going to visit that district again, so there was not the same danger in his becoming known. Decapolis (verse 20) was a district east of the Jordan which contained ten cities (as the name literally means) which were associated in government.

JAIRUS' DAUGHTER (verses 21–43)
  (Matt. ix. 18–26. Luke viii. 40–56)

Jesus was asked by Jairus to come and heal his daughter. On the way he was delayed by a woman suffering from haemorrhage, and the girl was reported to be dead. On arrival at Jairus' house, he took three disciples with him and raised the daughter up.

Jairus is called a ruler (N.E.B.: president) of the synagogue. In this office he would have care of the building and the arrangements connected with the wor-

ship on the Sabbath, and would select the readers
for the lessons. He was not a separated official but a
layman—possibly a local businessman who was prominent in the community. Mark does not say where these
incidents took place, except that Jesus and his company
had again crossed the lake (verse 21); it was presumably
in Galilee, perhaps in the neighbourhood of Capernaum.

The story of the healing of the woman (verses 25–34)
is dovetailed into the narrative. This may be the arrangement made by Mark, somewhat similar to the
way in which he interrupted the account of the visit of
Jesus' family (iii. 20–21, 31–35) with the story of the
scribes' accusation, and inserted the account of the
death of John the baptist between the sending out of
the twelve and their return (vi. 14–29).

The statement that the woman had spent much on
doctors (verse 26) suggests that she was of some means;
doctors were an expensive luxury in those days. Her
thought that she had only to touch Jesus' clothes in
order to be cured (verse 28) reflects the popular belief
that anything associated with a healer had power in
itself. Mark does not hesitate to ascribe ignorance to
Jesus—he asked who had touched him, a question
which the disciples thought rather pointless, in view of
the crowd around him (verses 30–31). Mark's frankness
is similarly shown in his statement that the people
jeered at Jesus in Jairus' house when he declared that
the girl was only asleep (verse 40).

On their arrival at Jairus' house, Peter, James and
John went aside with Jesus—the first time this inner
circle is mentioned (see also ix. 2; xiii. 3; xiv. 33). The
people who were weeping and wailing (verse 38) were
either professional mourners (although there would

hardly have been time for them to be called in) or members of the household giving vent to their grief. A message had been brought on the way to Jairus' house that the girl was dead (verse 35) but Jesus had made no comment (one translation of verse 36 is 'he ignored the message') except to tell Jairus not to be afraid but to have faith. At the house Jesus said that the girl was not dead but asleep. Some people think that Jesus meant the 'sleep of death'. But a different Greek word would be used for this and such a statement would have little point here. The people in the house evidently understood Jesus to mean that she was still alive; and he had made the definite statement: 'She is not dead.' Perhaps the girl had already recovered from her illness and Jesus knew, through 'second sight', that she was now sleeping peacefully. His word to her, 'Get up, my child' (verse 41–N.E.B.) might mean simply that she was to rise up from the bed.

Mark preserves the Aramaic words—*Talitha cum(i)*. Early Christians would greatly value such phrases which were actually on the lips of Jesus. Aramaic was the popular language of Palestine, a Syrian tongue written in Hebrew characters. Jesus gave his usual injunction to the people not to tell anyone about the occurrence (verse 43) but this would be useless in this case. Mark seems to have added this as a somewhat conventional comment.

CHAPTER VI

FURTHER GALILEAN ACTIVITIES

JESUS' VISIT TO NAZARETH (verses 1–6)
(Matt. xiii. 53–58. Luke iv. 16–30)

Jesus came to his own town and spoke in the synagogue, but the people were reluctant to accept his message because they were familiar with him and his family, so he was unable to do much among them.

Jesus may have been on a tour of Galilean towns and villages and in the course of it came to 'his own country' (N.E.B.: his own town). It seems obvious that Mark means Nazareth, although he does not name the place. The Greek word used here generally means a man's native place; perhaps Mark thought that Jesus had been born here and not, as Matthew and Luke state, at Bethlehem.

The attitude of the people when they heard Jesus speak in the synagogue is quite understandable. They knew him as a local artisan. The word used here means a craftsman in wood, stone or metal—generally a joiner or carpenter. There is no suggestion that they scorned him on the grounds of the poverty or low social position of himself or his family; there was little class-prejudice among the Jews and the carpenter would be a useful and respected member of the community. Their unwillingness to accept him sprang from the fact that he was a local man, whose mother and brothers and sisters were among them.

The question 'Is not this the carpenter?' (verse 3) is our authority for thinking that Jesus himself carried on Joseph's occupation, presumably after his father's death (although some manuscripts and versions have: 'Is not this the son of the carpenter and Mary?'). This is the only place where the names of his brothers are given and where mention is made of the fact that he had sisters also. James later became a disciple (probably after the resurrection) and was the leader of the church at Jerusalem; he is mentioned in the Acts and in Paul's letters. Because of his strict adherence to the Jewish Law, he became known as James the Just or the Righteous. He was put to death in the Temple court by the Jews in A.D. 62. Judas (or Jude) also joined the church. Nothing is known of his other brothers or of his sisters but Luke includes his mother and his brothers among those who gathered in Jerusalem with the apostles (Acts i. 14). Mark has already referred to them in iii. 31.

In his statement about a prophet in his own country (verse 4) Jesus appears to have been quoting a current proverb. A collection of the sayings of Jesus on papyrus found at Oxyrhynchus in Egypt contains this: 'A prophet is not accepted in his own country and a doctor does not work cures on those who know him.' Mark bluntly states that Jesus could not do any 'works of power' there, adding as an afterthought that a few sick folk were healed (verse 5). Jesus' power was evidently dependent on the faith or confidence of those with whom he dealt. Mark says that Jesus was surprised to find this lacking at Nazareth (verse 6). This suggests not only wonder on his part but also disappointment at his reception. He had apparently hoped for better things from his own townspeople.

There is no mention in the Gospels of any further visit to Nazareth. Luke iv. 16–30 gives a fuller account of what is presumably the same occasion, but from another source.

THE MISSION OF THE TWELVE DISCIPLES (verses 7–13)
(Matt. x. 5–42. Luke ix. 1–6)

Jesus summoned the twelve and sent them out on a preaching tour, with instructions on their message and their behaviour.

This commission of Jesus was recorded also in the document Q (reproduced in Luke x. 2ff.). The writer of Matthew's Gospel conflated Mark with the Q account and so compiled a long discourse of Jesus (Matt. x. 5ff.).

The disciples were evidently sent on only a short tour, not making provision for an extensive journey. The wandering teacher would be a familiar figure to Jesus' contemporaries and also to the first readers of Mark's Gospel. The messengers of the religious teacher in the East would receive a welcome from the people, who would give them board and lodging. They would carry a staff and a wallet and only such provisions as they needed for their journey to the next town or village. The disciples of Jesus were forbidden to take luggage or to carry a wallet or bag (N.E.B.: pack) (verse 8). The Greek word here is one which was used for a bag which the professional beggar in the Hellenistic world carried, for people to put money in. The disciples were told to accept hospitality but to reject any place which would not welcome them (verse 11). To shake the dust off one's feet was a symbolic gesture meaning 'We have nothing to do with you now.' The disciples preached repentance, exorcised possessed people and anointed the sick with oil, a common practice among doctors in the East.

The Imprisonment and Death of John the Baptist (verses 14–29)
(Matt. xiv. 1–12)

John had denounced the marriage of Herod Antipas with the wife of his half-brother. John was imprisoned for this but, after the daughter of Herodias had pleased Herod at a banquet, he had John beheaded on the demand of his wife.

While the disciples are away on their preaching tour, Mark takes the opportunity to tell further of John the baptist, introducing this by relating popular opinions about Jesus—that some thought he was Elijah or a prophet (cf. viii. 28, where these opinions are reported to Jesus himself). Elijah was expected to return to earth before the coming of the kingdom of God or the Messiah; the idea was based on Mal. iii. 1 and iv. 5. Herod thought that Jesus was John the baptist; his remark probably meant no more than: 'This is John all over again.'

Herod Antipas was one of the sons of Herod the Great and on his father's death he was appointed to rule Galilee and Perea. Mark calls him a king but his official title was tetrarch—literally a ruler of a fourth part of a kingdom. He reigned until A.D. 39, when he asked the emperor Caligula for the title of king but was banished and died in exile at Lyons. He had married the daughter of Aretas, king of Arabia (whose capital was Damascus) but he divorced her and took Herodias, the wife of one of his half-brothers. Mark says this man's name was Philip (verse 17) but he may have been confusing him with Philip the tetrarch of Iturea (north-east of Galilee). The Jewish historian Josephus calls him simply Herod and says he lived in Rome. John's rebuke to Antipas was based on the Old Testament law which stated that a man might not marry his sister-in-law during his brother's lifetime (Lev. xviii. 16; xx. 21). There was also a law forbidding a man to marry his niece. Herodias was the niece of each of the Herods.

Josephus also tells of the imprisonment of John but says it was in the castle of Machaerus in Perea. He does not mention John's denunciation of Herod's marriage but states that Herod put John in prison because he feared a revolt among the people, stirred up by John's preaching. He also says that Aretas went to war against Antipas and defeated him and that this was considered by many Jews to be a retribution for his execution of John.

The narrative of John's death (verses 21–29) is unlike any other passage in the Gospels. There is nothing in it about Jesus or his disciples and it was not part of the Christian 'gospel'. It seems to be a piece of popular report, which reached Mark by what channel we cannot say. The occasion was Herod's birthday feast, at which he was apparently adopting the Roman fashion of inter-spersing the courses of the meal with entertainment. This was generally provided by slaves and it would seem an undignified proceeding for a Jewish princess to dance before such a company. Josephus says the girl's name was Salome; she might be between twelve and fifteen years old at the time. She later married Philip, tetrarch of Iturea, her great-uncle.

The celebration may have been at Tiberias, on the lake of Galilee, which was Herod's capital. The 'lords and high captains' (verse 21: 'chief officials and commanders'–N.E.B.) who were present would be local officials and political officers. Herodias suggested the head of John as a present to her daughter, who added that it should be brought on a 'charger'—a dish or platter (verse 25). This was perhaps suggested by the sight of the dishes being carried into the feast—a gruesome whimsey.

This is the last mention in Mark of John's disciples (verse 29; cf. ii. 18), but there is evidence elsewhere that they did not disband after the death of their master but continued to reverence him.

THE RETURN OF THE DISCIPLES AND THE FEEDING OF FIVE THOUSAND PEOPLE (verses 30–44)
(Matt. xiv. 13–21. Luke ix. 10–17)

The twelve came back from their mission and Jesus suggested a period of retirement. But a crowd followed him around the lake and at the end of the day they were all fed.

Mark here calls the twelve 'apostles' (verse 30); this is probably the only place in this Gospel where the word appears (the reading in iii. 14 is doubtful). Here it means simply those who had been 'sent out' by him. The word was in general use in the first century for a messenger or delegate. Jesus now apparently desired a period of quiet with the twelve, perhaps to receive their reports of their mission, so he sought to withdraw from the crowds in the neighbourhood of Capernaum. Mark does not say where the 'desert place' (R.V.) was to which they went (verse 32); the phrase means simply a lonely spot, not a wilderness. It was evidently within a fairly short distance from Capernaum, for the people walked there, going around the shore of the lake, while Jesus and the disciples went by boat, and arrived before they disembarked. There were villages and small farms (verse 36–N.E.B.) not far off. The district may have been to the south-west of the lake.

The sum of money considered by the disciples to be sufficient to feed such a crowd (verse 37) was 200 denarii. A denarius was a silver coin which represented a day's wage for a labourer. The mention of green grass (verse 39) suggests that it was springtime but there is no indication whether or not this was the same spring as in ii. 23, when the ears of corn were ripe. Jesus acted as the host, for the usual action at the commencement of a meal was to bless the food (verse 41). It was presumably the disciples who had the loaves and fish (verse 38). This may have been all that was left of the food with which they had provided themselves on setting out that morning. This food would be carried in a basket of wicker-work; these were used afterwards for picking up the scraps (verse 43). The Roman poet Juvenal speaks scornfully of the Jew as the man whose whole household consisted of 'a basket [*cophinus*—the Latin equivalent of the Greek word used here] and a bundle of straw'.

There are various ways of regarding this incident. The traditional view has been that it was a 'miracle of creation'—that Jesus multiplied five loaves and two fishes to make enough to satisfy this large crowd. Mark appears to have regarded it as such, although he does not actually say so and does not indicate at what point each loaf became two or each fish became several. There is, however, no suggestion or other evidence in the New Testament that Jesus was able to create material things, and the picture in the Gospels is of one who was subject to human physical limitations. Such a stupendous feat would moreover have been convincing proof of Jesus' power and authority but this is never referred to either by friends or enemies. Such an action would also appear to be contrary to Jesus' resolve at the beginning of his work, when he was tempted to turn stones into bread—to be the kind of Messiah who would feed the people (Luke iv. 3; Matt. iv. 3). He consistently refused to supply signs and wonders (cf. Mark viii. 12).

Some have suggested that Jesus held a feast in anticipation of a gathering in the kingdom of God, which was often pictured by the Jews under the figure of a messianic banquet. On this view he distributed only small morsels of food. This was a material symbol of the spiritual nourishment which the people received from his teaching. But the statement in verse 42 that they were all satisfied is against this. Others think that the numbers are the unhistorical element in the story, that it was originally an account of a meal with the twelve on a few loaves and fishes and became magnified in tradition into a feeding of five thousand people.

In seeking to reconstruct the scene we may consider that no crowd in the East would go out into the country for a day without taking provisions, any more than we should ourselves. Jews always took their food with them, as this had to be specially prepared. The disciples had some still—the loaves and fish would be enough for a light meal—and it is unlikely that the rest of the crowd would have eaten all their provisions before the end of the day. So Jesus may have got the disciples, after arranging the people in convenient groups (verse 40), to go among them and distribute the food which they themselves had. They then found that there was not only enough to go round but also some to spare. It might be said that this was indeed a 'miracle'—that under the influence of Jesus people who were naturally selfish found that when they shared they were all satisfied.

THE CROSSING OF THE LAKE (verses 45–56)
(Matt. xiv. 22–36)

The disciples started across the lake of Galilee, while Jesus remained behind. In the early morning he joined them in their boat.

Mark says that the disciples set out for Bethsaida. This was Bethsaida Julias, a town to the north of the lake, near the point where the Jordan enters it. It had been built by Herod Philip and named in honour of Julia, the daughter of the emperor Augustus. But, instead of arriving there, the boat is said to have reached Gennesaret (verse 53); this was a plain extending three miles along the lakeside, to the south of Capernaum. Bethsaida is not reached until viii. 22—obviously not at the completion of this journey here, for many events had happened in the meantime, in Galilee and Phoenicia.

Not only the geography but the time of this incident is also confused. The day was ending when the disciples called Jesus' attention to the condition of the crowd (vi. 35); it was evening when the disciples embarked (verse 47). Yet Mark states that it was early morning when they saw Jesus (verse 48). The fourth watch was from 3 to 6 a.m. The Romans divided the night into four watches, the Jews into three. Mark is writing for Gentiles and so uses their reckoning. They could hardly have spent all the intervening time rowing across the lake. Mark says they were 'in the midst of the sea' (verse 47 R.V.; N.E.B.: 'Well out on the water'). But the lake is only six miles at its greatest breadth. All this confusion suggests that this was originally an independent story which Mark has placed here for want of a better position. Perhaps it is a variant account of the incident in iv. 35–41.

Popularly Jesus is thought of as overcoming the force of gravitation and walking across the surface of the lake. There seems no reason why he should take a 'short cut' across the water, apart from the fact that such a power of levitation is not attributed to him elsewhere. Consequently some think that Jesus was walking along the shore towards Bethsaida, intending to join the disciples there. In view of their previous experience, they were probably keeping close to the shore. Seeing Jesus, they were surprised, for they had last seen him going into the hills to pray (verse 46). Jesus intended to pass them by (verse 48) but they caught sight of him. To quell their fear, he came towards them, walking in the shallow water.

Other suggestions have been that the disciples had a vision of Jesus, although he was actually still praying in the hills, or that the story is a symbolic dramatisation of the belief of the early disciples that Jesus was with them in their troubles as they rowed against the contrary winds of this world.

Mark concludes the incident with an obscure reference to the lesson of the loaves (verse 52), suggesting some hidden meaning in the incident of the feeding of the people which the disciples had missed, but he does not make it clear what this was. The final paragraph (verses 53–56) is a general statement of Jesus' popularity in Galilee and his acts of healing. It closes this section of the Gospel (chaps. i–vi).

CHAPTER VII

FURTHER OPPOSITION AND JOURNEYS OUTSIDE GALILEE

A Dispute About Scribal Tradition (verses 1–23)
(Matt. xv. 1–20)

Pharisees complained that Jesus' disciples neglected the traditions of the elders by eating food with defiled hands. In defending them, Jesus attacked the Pharisees' adherence to these traditions, pointing out that they nullified Old Testament commandments, and explained to the disciples what constituted real defilement—a man's inner thoughts.

This passage starts with another conflict-story, resuming the theme of chapters ii–iii. But wider issues soon emerge. The initial complaint was that the disciples ate their food without the thorough ritual washing which was customary among strict Jews. Jesus gives his reply to this attack in verses 6–8 and 9–13, ignoring the charge against the disciples but making instead an attack on the Pharisees with their lip-service to God and their adherence to the traditions. He then deals with the question of what constitutes 'defilement' (verses 14–15), addressing the people in general, and in verses 18–23 he explains this teaching to the disciples. Mark has probably brought together here some teaching which was given on different occasions.

The 'traditions of the elders' were additions to the Old Testament and constituted the 'oral Law', placed by the Pharisees on the same level as the written Law which was attributed to Moses. It was held that these traditions had been handed down from the earliest times of Hebrew history. They were preserved and transmitted by the scribes, who thus sought to include the whole range of human conduct within the regulations and to give guidance to all situations in everyday life.

The word 'defiled' (verse 2) means strictly secular or profane, as opposed to holy or consecrated. Because they might have been in contact in their business with Gentiles or other people outside the Law, the strict Pharisees took particular care to wash their hands thoroughly, in a special ceremonial way. Mark exaggerates when he says 'all the Jews' did such things (verse 3). Although a Jew himself, he here associates himself with the point of view of his Gentile readers. The cups referred to were drinking vessels, the pots or jugs were pitchers holding about a pint. Even today the strict Jew has his own special household utensils and will not have his food cooked in a vessel belonging to a Gentile.

The first part of Jesus' reply (verses 6–8) does not deal directly with the point at issue but rebukes the Jews who pay only lip-service to God, not true worship, which is from the heart. The quotation is from Isa. xxix. 13. The statement that Isaiah 'prophesied' in this passage about the Pharisees does not mean that he foretold the existence of the sect but simply that their conduct was an illustration of the prophet's words.

In his second answer (verses 9–13) Jesus attacked the rules such as the ritual washing as mere 'traditions of men' and showed that the consequences of adhering to them might lead to the putting aside of the ten commandments, which all Jews considered binding. As an illustration he mentioned the practice of 'corban', which was held to have precedence over the honouring of one's parents. Corban is a transliteration of an Aramaic word meaning an offering or a gift. A man might swear that his goods were dedicated to God and might then say that it was impossible for him to make use of the money or goods to help his parents. The Jewish rabbis were divided on the question how far an oath of this kind was binding, if it meant neglect of the Law. The Old Testament was strict about keeping one's oaths, so the pious Jew was in a dilemma. The practice might also furnish an excuse for an unworthy son to cease caring for his parents. Jesus said that the commandment should come first.

The rest of the passage (verses 14–23) consists of a statement to the crowd (verses 14–15) and an explanation delivered privately to the disciples (verses 16–23). (This is the same idea as is found in iv. 10ff. and iv. 33ff.) The original cause of the complaint in verse 5 is now lost sight of, for the statement in verse 15 has little bearing on this controversy. It was probably an independent saying of Jesus. It is very sweeping (and is amplified in verses 18–19), setting aside the food laws which were an essential part of Judaism. Mark himself perceived this when he added 'Thus he declared all foods clean' (verse 19). It is difficult to think that Jesus spoke in this way. If he had, such a remark could have been quoted in the controversy in the early Church about the enforcement of Jewish regulations upon Gentile converts and would have settled the matter, whereas we find Peter indignantly repudiating the suggestion that he should eat anything 'common or unclean' (Acts x. 14). The statement in Mark is probably the result of later Christian reflection on Jesus' spirit and teaching and its application to the problems of the writer's own time.

The list in verses 21–23 of the things that really 'defile' a man—his inward thoughts and impulses—is reminiscent of the lists of vices of the Gentile world in some of Paul's letters and is probably a Christian interpretation and amplification of Jesus' general principle. But they nevertheless do reflect the basic idea in his teaching—that what is important is not so much a man's acts as his inward motive and state of mind.

A VISIT TO PHOENICIA (verses 24–30)
(Matt. xv. 21–28)

Jesus and the disciples retired to Phoenicia, where a woman asked him to heal her daughter. After an exchange of remarks about the food of the children and the dogs, Jesus told her to return home and find her daughter cured.

A new section of Mark's Gospel begins here, where he deals with Jesus' activities in the north but outside Galilee (vii. 24 to ix. 29). Tyre and Sidon, both seaports on the Mediterranean coast, were the chief towns of the country of Phoenicia. In the first century A.D. this was part of the Roman province of Syria but it had had a long history as an independent country. It is to the Phoenicians that we owe ultimately our alphabet. In the ninth century B.C. Jezebel, daughter of the king of Tyre, had married Ahab, king of Israel, with disastrous consequences for the people of this northern kingdom. The Phoenicians were a great trading people and founded colonies along the coast of north Africa and in Spain. They founded Carthage in north Africa, which was destroyed by the Romans in 146 B.C.

Jesus' stay in Phoenicia was the only occasion during

the course of his ministry when he visited a 'foreign' country. He appears to have been seeking privacy (verse 24) and perhaps wished to receive reports from his disciples about their mission tour. He had been frustrated earlier in this purpose by the crowds who had pursued him round the lake (vi. 31). But even in Phoenicia he was apparently known and was sought out by a woman who is described as 'a Greek, a Syro-Phoenician by birth'. This means she was a Gentile (as N.E.B.). 'Phoenician' designates her race and 'Syro-' indicates that she lived in the Roman province of Syria. She would be a pagan, not worshipping the Jewish God. The conversation between her and Jesus would probably be carried on in Greek, for this was the common language which was general throughout the Roman world. We may conclude that Jesus was bilingual. Among his fellow-Jews he would use Aramaic, the language of Palestine, but he could converse with a foreigner in Greek.

Jesus' response to the woman's request, that the children's food should not be thrown to dogs (verse 28), seems harsh and strange on his lips. The Jews referred to Gentiles as dogs and thought of themselves as the children of God. But the Greek word which is used here is not the word of contempt for the scavenger dog of the East but a diminutive—'little dogs'. Mark is rather fond of such forms, so too much must not be read into it here; but it is probable that a gentler tone was implied by Jesus' remark. The dogs to which the woman referred (verse 28) were obviously household dogs, crouching under the table at meal-times. Possibly Jesus, pondering over his work in relation to Jews and Gentiles, uttered the remarks under his breath and the woman overheard him. Another suggestion is that the woman was the

first to mention 'dogs', knowing how Jews regarded her
people, and Jesus responded to the words that she had
used.

Mark says that Jesus complied with the woman's
request because of her saying (verse 29); he was presumably pleased with her wit and her readiness to take a
subordinate place. Mark does not actually state that
Jesus cured the girl, only that he told the mother to go
home and she would find the girl well. Cure at a distance, with the patient unaware of the healer's efforts
and unable to take any part, seems difficult to accept. It
has accordingly been suggested that Jesus knew, by
'second sight', that the girl had recovered. The woman
took him at his word and found that it was so.

THE CURE OF A DEAF STAMMERER (verses 31–37)

*Returning to Galilee through Decapolis, Jesus took aside a deaf
man who had an impediment in his speech and, using Aramaic
words and saliva, restored him.*

The route indicated in verse 31 is very strange. Sidon
was twenty miles north of Tyre, the lake of Galilee was
south-east of Phoenicia, and Decapolis ('the territory of
the Ten Towns'–N.E.B.) was east of the Jordan. It is
equivalent to saying that a man left Chester and went
through Manchester to Birmingham by way of Oxford.
It seems that the writer was not very familiar with the
geography of northern Palestine.

The cure of this man is one of two miracles of healing
which are found only in Mark; the other is the story of a
blind man at Bethsaida (viii. 22–26), which is somewhat
like this one. The other two Synoptic writers omitted
these perhaps because they did not like the thought of
Jesus' using material means to effect a cure. The term

used to describe the man's trouble (verse 32) translated 'with an impediment in his speech' is one Greek word which means 'speaking with difficulty'. The statement that he 'spoke plainly' (verse 35) also suggests not dumbness but a defect in his speech. Saliva was supposed then to have healing properties. Jesus' actions in using this and in touching the man's tongue are similar to those of Jewish and Greek healers of the time. Mark preserves the Aramaic word used by Jesus (verse 34), as he does in the case of Jairus' daughter (v. 41), and there follows the usual injunction to silence, but without much effect (cf. i. 44–45).

CHAPTER VIII

ON THE WAY TO CAESAREA PHILIPPI

THE FEEDING OF FOUR THOUSAND PEOPLE (verses 1–10)
(Matt. xv. 29–39)

*A crowd spent three days with Jesus in the country and then four
thousand were fed.*

Mark gives no indication where this incident happened. Jesus is last stated to have been passing through
Decapolis (vii. 31), which was the district east of the
Jordan, on the way back to Galilee. After the people
had been fed he sailed to Dalmanutha (verse 10), but
the site of this place is quite unknown. The next town
mentioned is Bethsaida, north of the lake (verse 22),
for which the disciples had set out after the feeding of
the five thousand (vi. 45). In this section (verses 1–26)
Mark seems to have brought together a number of
incidents which were originally not related geographi-
cally or chronologically.

There are other features also in this narrative of the
feeding which are vague and confused. The crowd is
said to have been with Jesus for three days (verse 2) but
there is no hint where the people had lived or how they
had fed during that time. The narrative is very similar
to that of the feeding of the five thousand. The disciples
ask similar questions, how the people are to be fed (vi.
35–37 and viii. 4). In reply Jesus asks them how many
loaves they have (vi. 38; viii. 5) and gives them the

same instructions, to get the people to sit down (vi. 40; viii. 6). In both instances the disciples distribute food (vi. 41; viii. 6–7). Jesus blesses it (vi. 41; viii. 7) and the fragments are collected (vi. 43; viii. 8). The crowd is then dismissed (vi. 45; viii. 9) and the disciples and Jesus take a boat and cross the lake (vi. 45; viii. 10). The disciples here show no knowledge of any earlier occasion with a similar predicament or any anticipation of what Jesus would do about it. The conclusion generally arrived at is that these are two accounts of the same occasion. The story of the five thousand seems to be the more primitive account. The second narrative is bare, compared with it. The few details added (verses 2–3) are the kind of amplification which would become attached to such a story when it was told. This applies also to the variation in the number of the people and of the loaves and fishes. A different Greek word is also used for the baskets in which the fragments were collected. The one here (verse 7) is a wicker basket for carrying provisions; Paul was let down over the wall of Damascus in one such (Acts ix. 25).

THE DEMAND FOR A SIGN (verses 11–13)
(Matt. xvi. 1–4)

The Pharisees asked Jesus for a 'sign' but he refused to give one.

The Pharisees may have wanted some demonstration from Jesus of his authority. Many Jews were eagerly looking for the coming of a new age, which would be heralded by signs and wonders, and Jesus' questioners may have been thinking of these. Jesus had proclaimed that the kingdom of God was at hand; what proof had he to give them?

If the feeding of the people had just taken place, as Mark says it had, Jesus could surely have referred to such a miracle as sufficient for friends and opponents alike. The Pharisees' demand and Jesus' refusal to give any sign suggest that it had not been a miraculous feeding of a large crowd from a few loaves and fish.

THE SIGNIFICANCE OF THE LOAVES (verses 14–21)
(Matt. xvi. 5–12)

When the disciples were disturbed because they had not much food with them, Jesus warned them against the influence of the Pharisees and of Herod and rebuked them because they did not understand the significance of the feeding of the people.

This is one of the most perplexing passages in the Gospels. The disciples' discussion about lack of bread, which is mentioned in verses 14 and 16, is interrupted by a warning of Jesus about the Pharisees and Herod (verse 15). Leaven is yeast, which is added to the flour to make bread rise. It generally has a bad name in the Bible and stands for a hidden but powerful influence. This remark might be regarded as an 'aside', if spoken by Jesus here, but it is more probable that it is a statement made on another occasion, which has been inserted here by Mark. It might well have come after the mention of the plot by Pharisees and Herodians (iii. 6). The disciples are represented as being dull (verses 17–18)—not for the first time in this Gospel (cf. iv. 13; vii. 18)—but the answer to Jesus' questions is not given and it is not at all clear to us what they were expected to understand. Possibly Jesus meant they should have been able to appreciate that he could supply their deepest needs; why should they worry therefore about lack of material bread, which was comparatively unimportant?

Another suggestion is that Mark's contemporaries in the Church saw special significance in the stories of the feeding of the people and related it to the Lord's Supper with which they were familiar. Mark points out that the disciples did not discern this at the time.

Verses 19–20 associate the two feedings and compare the amount of food and the fragments taken up afterwards. These are, however, generally regarded as variant accounts of the same incident and these verses are hence treated as composed by Mark himself or some earlier Christian teacher who was trying to bring out what he thought was Jesus' message. Jesus may have reminded the disciples in general terms of the meals which they had shared together and his sayings were put in this form.

THE CURE OF A BLIND MAN (verses 22–26)

At Bethsaida a blind man, brought to Jesus, was taken aside and treated in two stages before he recovered his full sight.

This is the second miracle told only by Mark, the other being the cure of the deaf stammerer (vii. 32–37). It is similar in the means employed (the use of saliva and the touching of the afflicted parts with Jesus' hands) and in the words he used and in the way in which the man was taken aside by Jesus. This man was apparently not blind from birth, for he knew what trees looked like (verse 24) when Jesus asked him if he could see anything. Perhaps he was not completely blind and Jesus was asking him if he could normally see anything. He replied that he could already recognise things like trees, which he assumed were men. In this case the cure was not, as is generally supposed, a gradual one, performed in two stages, but came about when the man 'saw everything clearly' (verse 25).

Bethsaida, for which the disciples had set out after the feeding of the five thousand (vi. 45), was in the territory of Herod Philip, outside Galilee and north of the lake. This sets the scene for the narrative which follows.

JESUS AND THE DISCIPLES NEAR CAESAREA PHILIPPI (verses 27–33)
(Matt. xvi. 13–23. Luke ix. 18–22)

Jesus asked the disciples what people thought of him. After receiving their replies, he put the question to them and Peter declared he was the Messiah. Jesus then spoke of the suffering of the Son of Man and Peter was sternly rebuked when he protested at the idea.

Caesarea Philippi was called by this double name to distinguish it from Caesarea on the Mediterranean coast. It had formerly been called Paneas, for there was a grotto there sacred to the god Pan. Herod the Great had built a temple nearby, in honour of the emperor Augustus. The city had been rebuilt and renamed by Herod Philip, one of the sons of Herod the Great. It was about twenty-five miles north of Bethsaida, from which the journey may have started. Mark does not say the company actually went into the city but that they were visiting the villages in the neighbourhood.

Jesus first asked the disciples for the popular opinions about him. The answers reported (verse 28) are those which Mark has already mentioned (vi. 14). Jesus appeared to some to be 'John the baptist all over again', while others thought that he was an incarnation of Elijah (that is, a prophet with the same spirit as Elijah had shown), who was supposed to be coming before the establishment of the kingdom of God. There was evidently no suggestion that Jesus might be the Messiah, for he was obviously so unlike the Messiah expected by the Jews. 'Demon-possessed' people had previously declared Jesus to be 'God's holy one' or 'God's son' but he had ordered them to be silent (i. 25; iii. 11–12). When Peter declared, in answer to Jesus' second question, that Jesus was the Messiah, it was the first time that the actual term had been applied to him. Possibly Peter spoke for the rest of the disciples, who may have already discussed the question among themselves.

The word Messiah (the Greek for which is Christ) means 'anointed'. It was used in the Old Testament of kings, who were anointed with oil when they ascended the throne, and later of priests and prophets. It is not used in the Old Testament as a proper name, designating a future king. This idea became more prominent in the Jewish apocalyptic books of the first and second centuries B.C. The writers thought that God would intervene in the midst of calamity and tragedy and establish his kingdom of righteousness. The Messiah was to be his agent in this. In the minds of many of Jesus' contemporaries the hope of political freedom was associated with this expectation. Jesus was evidently not like the conventional Messiah, a figure of glory and power, so Peter's statement showed some advance and that he at any rate was able to conceive of a different kind of Messiah. Yet even he felt bound to protest when Jesus went on to speak about suffering and death (verses 31–32). Perhaps his words recalled to Jesus the temptations which he had undergone before commencing his work; he was again being urged to take the wrong way to demonstrate his messiahship; hence the fierceness of his rebuke to Peter (verse 33), when he addressed him as 'Satan'; the term would mean simply an adversary—its original meaning.

Jesus now gave to the disciples the command to silence which he had given to the demons (verse 30). In Mark's Gospel the messiahship of Jesus is regarded as a secret which was not disclosed by Jesus until he was challenged by the high priest at his trial (xiv. 61–62). Jesus' instructions are then followed by his prediction of what was to meet him at Jerusalem. There are three of these statements in Mark (viii. 31; ix. 31; x. 33–34). Each time the wording becomes more precise in its details about his suffering, rejection by the leaders of the Jews and his death. But if Jesus spoke in such definite terms about his fate, it is difficult to see why the disciples were so dismayed and panic-stricken when it did come about. This makes one suspicious of the wording which is attributed to him. It is certainly likely that Jesus did foresee, especially towards the end of his ministry, where the opposition of his enemies would lead, and realised the danger he was running in going to Jerusalem and warned his disciples in advance. But the actual wording given in the Gospels was probably influenced by the writers' knowledge of what actually happened. In the light of events, Mark made Jesus' statements more specific than they were.

Each statement ends with a prediction of a resurrection 'after three days'. This was a Hebrew phrase meaning 'in a short time'. But the accounts in the Gospels show that the disciples were entirely unprepared for this after the crucifixion. The women on the way to the tomb, to anoint Jesus' dead body, had no such hope (Mark xvi. 1ff.) and the disciples did not believe the report of Jesus' resurrection when it was

brought to them (Luke xxiv. 11; xxiv. 23–24; cf. John
xx. 25). These facts suggest that Jesus did not speak so
definitely as he is here represented. He probably spoke
in general terms of his treatment at Jerusalem and his
ultimate triumph after apparent defeat, but his words
were overlooked or misunderstood by the disciples.
Perhaps they were still thinking in terms of Jewish
apocalyptic ideas and hoped for the manifestation of
the Son of Man in glory in the heavens. Jesus' general
warnings and expectations were expressed afterwards
in the tradition in more definite terms, as we find them
recorded in the Gospels.

In uttering these predictions, however, Jesus did
not use the term Messiah, which Peter had employed,
but spoke of the suffering and rejection of the Son of
Man.[1] This term has occurred in Mark only twice so
far—at ii. 10 ('the Son of Man has authority to forgive
sins') and ii. 28 ('the Son of Man is lord of the Sabbath'). But from this point onwards it comes frequently
on the lips of Jesus.

It seems that Jesus wished not to adopt the title
Messiah, which Peter had used, and forbade his disciples to proclaim it. To his contemporaries in Israel
it would suggest a triumphant rebel leader, who would
lead the people against the rule of Rome and establish
an independent state, which would nevertheless be
ruled by God himself. Instead, he deliberately chose
the term Son of Man, as representing mankind and
above all the true Israel which, like the martyrs who
had been persecuted by the foreign ruler, gained its
triumph through suffering. It was this thought which
drew forth Peter's protest, since he was thinking of

[1] See p. 27 for an account of the meaning of the term in the Old Testament and later literature.

triumph through force and glory. Jesus probably had also in mind the picture of the suffering servant of God in the second part of Isaiah (especially Isa. liii).

TEACHING ON SERVICE AND SACRIFICE (verses 34–38 and ix. 1)
(Matt. xvi. 24–28. Luke ix. 22–27)

Jesus told the crowd that they must be prepared to lose their lives in order to gain real life and spoke of the coming of the Son of Man and the kingdom of God.

These statements are said to have been delivered to a crowd which Jesus called to him (verse 34). This seems unlikely in this situation, for Jesus had been alone with the disciples in the district of Caesarea Philippi, having left the Galilean crowds which generally followed him. Mark has probably placed here a number of sayings which may have been delivered on other occasions; Mark thought them suitable here, to follow Jesus' words about his own sufferings. The metaphor about taking up a cross (verse 34) was a grim one; such a man was on the way to execution, a fairly familiar sight in a province of the Roman empire. It would have special significance for Mark's readers, if he wrote for the church at Rome, who were suffering under Nero's persecution. The Roman historian Tacitus says that some of the Christians were nailed to crosses or were burnt. The statement about keeping and losing one's life (verse 35) expresses the paradox of self-sacrifice. The saying was also in the document Q (Luke xvii. 33; Matt. x. 39) and was probably repeated by Jesus on several occasions. Verse 38 seems to be an independent saying, with very little connection with what precedes here. The term Son of Man is used in

a different way. It reflects here the more conventional
idea of this figure in the first century. The 'figure
like a man' of Daniel had become in apocalyptic works
'the Son of Man' or 'the Man', who would appear
with God for the judgment of the world, to condemn
the wicked and to rule over the righteous and bring
in the messianic age. The thought seems at variance
with the conception of the suffering Son of Man de-
picted in the previous paragraph (verse 31); some
have suggested that Jesus did not mean himself when
he spoke in this way but was reproducing the popular
idea to emphasise the thought of judgment.

The first verse of chapter ix is part of this paragraph.
It may have come from a collection of sayings, beginning afresh with 'And he said'. It is a saying which
has caused much difficulty and received various
interpretations. In what sense was the coming of the
kingdom of God with power witnessed by those present
with Jesus? The prediction has been taken by some to
refer to the transfiguration, the account of which
follows immediately, and is said to have occurred six
days later. But it is difficult to see how this can be
regarded as a manifestation of God's kingdom; and it
would seem rather banal for Jesus to remark that some
of those who were with him would not die within a
week. Other suggestions have been that the resurrection of Jesus was referred to, or the gift of the Spirit
to the disciples. But these events are not thought of in
the New Testament as the coming of the kingdom.
Another idea has been that the statement referred to
the spread of Christianity in the world, but this seems
to be too general an interpretation.

A common way has been to take the saying as
referring to the coming of the Son of Man, following

on the statement about this in the previous verse. The early Christians expected the coming of Jesus in glory (or the *parousia*, as it is generally called now, using the Greek word for 'arrival') to take place within their own lifetime, and it is assumed that this verse was their authority for this view. If this is the meaning, we must conclude that Jesus made a mistake, for this appearance of the Son of Man did not happen during the lifetime of those present. C. H. Dodd suggested that the statement did not refer to a future coming of the kingdom at all, but to Jesus' proclamation of the kingdom as present there and then. He would translate the Greek: ' ... until they have seen that the kingdom of God has come with power'. The kingdom, said Jesus, had already arrived and some of those present would soon realise this.

The words may, however, not be those of Jesus but a comment added by a narrator or preacher. He wanted to assure those whom he was addressing that they would not die until they had seen fulfilled the prediction of the coming of the kingdom.

CHAPTER IX

RETURN FROM THE NORTH TO CAPERNAUM

The Transfiguration of Jesus (verses 2–13)
(Matt. xvii. 1–13. Luke ix. 28–36)

On a mountain, in the presence of three disciples, Jesus was changed in appearance and Moses and Elijah were seen with him. A voice declared him to be God's Son, to whom men were to listen. On descending the mountain Jesus explained to the disciples the significance of Elijah and the expectation of his coming.

Peter, James and John had already accompanied Jesus alone when he went into Jairus' house (v. 37) and here they were chosen to share a psychical or spiritual experience with Jesus. Most people today would find it difficult to accept the view, which is at any rate suggested by Mark's narrative, that Moses and Elijah were actually present, having come back to earth. The Jews had no pictures or sculpture of their ancient heroes, so it is pointless to ask how the disciples would recognise them, for they would not know what they looked like when on earth. This was evidently a vision which they had of Jesus in glory, in which he was associated with these Old Testament figures. Perhaps it acted as a confirmation of Peter's acknowledgment of him as Messiah at Caesarea Philippi.

The mountain where this is thought to have happened is uncertain. It is sometimes taken as Mount Tabor, but this was in Galilee. Another suggestion is Mount Hermon, which is twelve miles from Caesarea Philippi. The time is given by Mark with unusual exactness, as being 'after six days' (verse 2); but it is not clear whether this means six days after the events in viii. 27ff., or the teaching to the crowd in viii. 34ff., or the statement made in ix. 1. J. M. C. Crum suggested that Mark noticed at this point in his writing that he had collected material covering six days and remarked that this event happened after these six days.

Moses and Elijah are generally taken to represent Old Testament religion, Moses being the traditional founder of the Law and Elijah one of the earliest prophets; their appearance here was thus to show that Jesus was in accord with Judaism, in his teaching, as 'fulfilling' its precepts and spirit (cf. Matt. v. 17), and they disappeared while Jesus remained (verse 8). There was also the current expectation that Elijah would appear before the Messiah. There may be intended another link with Jesus in that both these men had suffered much at the hands of their contemporaries, so the vision may depict the disciples' realisation of the truth of Jesus' words about his way being that of suffering.

For the first time in Mark Jesus is addressed as 'Rabbi' (verse 5). This was a Hebrew word meaning 'my master'. The rabbi was a religious teacher who was expert in the Jewish Law. Strictly, Jesus was not a rabbi, for he had not been trained as a professional teacher. The word translated 'tabernacles' (R.V.) or 'shelters' (N.E.B.) is really 'tent', meaning a temporary dwelling-place. The Hebrews had lived in these during their

journey through the wilderness after leaving Egypt
under the guidance of Moses. Mark comments in a
typically blunt fashion on Peter's thoughtless remark,
that he did not know what to say (verse 6), an indication of Peter's impetuous nature and also of his
honesty, if the source of Mark's information was Peter
himself.

Coming down from the mountain, Jesus told the
disciples to keep quiet about their experience, but there
is some confusion in the report of their conversation
(verses 9–13). The remarks about the Son of Man
rising from the dead (verses 9–10) are interrupted by
a question about Elijah's coming and Jesus' answer
confirming this idea (verses 11–12a). The question
about the Son of Man is then resumed (verse 12b) but
it is not clear whether this was spoken by Jesus or the
disciples. The conversation then returns to the question
of Elijah (verse 13). It seems that there are reports
here of two conversations. One was about the fate of
the Son of Man. In reply to Jesus' injunction to
silence (verse 9), the disciples discussed his meaning
(verse 10) and asked him what was the basis in the
Old Testament for the idea of a suffering Son of Man
(verse 12b). There was actually no such basis for this,
for it was not written of the Son of Man that he would
suffer and be rejected. The conception was rather
that he would come in glory. But it was written that
the servant of Yahweh would suffer. The term Son of
Man seems again to be associated with the conception
of the Servant (as in viii. 31; cf. x. 45).

Interwoven with this conversation is the report of
another topic, about Elijah. The disciples asked a
question about Elijah's coming (verse 11) and Jesus
answered them (verses 12a and 13). Mark does not

make it clear who is referred to in the statement about Elijah as having already come (verse 13). It seems to refer to John the baptist, whose appearance has reminded people of Elijah (cf. i. 6), for he had suffered at the hands of Herod Antipas. The last part of verse 13, with its reference to the Old Testament, is probably a note by Mark himself. There was no scripture which said this about Elijah.

The Cure of an Epileptic (verses 14–29)
(Matt. xvii. 14–20. Luke ix. 37–43a)

Returning to the rest of the disciples, Jesus found them unable to cure a boy who had been brought to them by his father, who begged Jesus to cure his son, eventually expressing his belief that this could be done. The boy had a fit, Jesus exorcised the demon and the sufferer was restored.

Mark may have put in verses 14–16 to link the incident with the transfiguration, if the original narrative, as an independent story, started with verse 17. The situation has seemed to some to be appropriate, to show the contrast between the glory of the transfiguration scene on the mountain and the realities of life on the plain beneath, but it is doubtful if this artistic effect was intended by Mark.

The narrative, although containing a certain amount of repetition, is very vivid, especially in the description of the features of epilepsy (from which the boy presumably suffered)—the attacks of speechlessness, falling to the ground and foaming at the mouth, the rigidity of the body and the final attack which made people think he was dead (verse 26). The fits were thought at that time to be due to demon-possession. The fire upon which the sufferer might fall (verse 22) would be burning on the open hearth in the Palestinian house; the water might be a river by which the boy was walking when a fit seized him. These statements of the father may indicate suicidal tendencies or may simply refer to the danger for an epileptic when in a fit.

The conversation between the father and Jesus is also very vividly told. Many translations obscure the play upon words which takes place in verses 22–24. Jesus first echoes the father's words of doubt—'If you can!' His next words—'[all things] are possible'—represent the same Greek verb. This is shown in the N.E.B. translation. Finally, Jesus gives a command to the sufferer, or the demon thought to be in him (verse 25)—his usual practice in healing people (cf. i. 25; ii. 11; iii. 5; v. 41). The boy apparently lost his hearing as well as his speech when the fit took him, for Jesus addressed the spirit as 'dumb and deaf'. The idea behind this was that the demon was one which lacked these faculties, so it 'borrowed' those of the boy, who was thus deprived of them.

The final conversation between Jesus and the disciples (verses 28–29) seems inappropriate; it is said to have taken place in a house (N.E.B.: 'indoors') but there is no indication whose house. Neither has there been any mention of prayer either before the incident or during the cure; and Mark does not say whose prayer is intended, Jesus' or the disciples'. The words were probably spoken in another connection. Later manuscripts of Mark added the words 'and fasting' to the mention of prayer, to accord with the practice of the Church later on.

SECOND STATEMENT OF THE PASSION (verses 30–32)
(Matt. xvii. 22–23. Luke ix. 43b–45)

*On the way through Galilee Jesus again spoke of the death
and resurrection of the Son of Man.*

Jesus was travelling incognito (verse 30), so that he
might not attract a crowd, as he wished to teach his
disciples privately. The wording here is similar to that
in vii. 31.

THE CHILD AS AN EXAMPLE (verses 33–37)
(Matt. xviii. 1–5. Luke ix. 46–48)

*The disciples were arguing about greatness, so Jesus talked
about service and set a child among them.*

The journey which started in verse 30 is continued,
the company having now arrived at Capernaum. The
discussion among the disciples may have been about
who was the most important of their company or, more
probably, who was to be the leader in the coming
kingdom which they expected Jesus to establish. Jesus'
answer to them is given in verse 35—the first must be
prepared to be the last and to serve. The rest of the
paragraph, which describes Jesus taking a child and
speaking about receiving a child, appears to have
nothing to do with the dispute of the disciples. There is
another incident involving children in x. 13–16. It
seems that the two stories have become confused, for
Jesus' statement there about the terms of entry into
the kingdom of God (x. 15) seems more applicable as
Jesus' answer to the disciples here. The remarks made
here about receiving a child (verse 37) are more
appropriate to the incident in chapter x.

THE DISCIPLES AND AN EXORCIST (verses 38–40)
(Luke ix. 49–50)

John wished to stop an exorcist because he was not one of their company, although he used the name of Jesus. Jesus told the disciples not to hinder such people who did good.

This is the only time in the Gospels that John speaks for himself, without his brother James. His intolerant outburst bears out the nickname 'son of thunder' given him by Jesus. There were people in the Jewish and Gentile worlds who attempted to cure sufferers whose maladies were ascribed to demon-possession. It was the practice for an exorcist to use some such formula as 'In the name of . . . ', when driving out a demon, calling to their aid the authority of a god or superior spirit or some man who was of a more powerful reputation than himself (cf. Acts xix. 13).

Jesus' statement in verse 40—'the one not against us is for us'—at first sight seems to contradict a Q saying: 'He who is not with me is against me' (Luke xi. 23; Matt. xii. 30). But there it is an appeal to an individual who might be tempted to be neutral. Here it expresses a principle laid down for Jesus' followers, in dealing with others about whose position they might have doubts. It is a plea for tolerance.

The occasion of John's demand to Jesus to stop the exorcist may have been earlier, on the return of the disciples from their preaching tour in Mark vi, when they were relating to Jesus the success of their work. Mark placed the incident here perhaps because of the words 'in your name' (verse 38) and 'in my name' (verse 39), which form a link with the words in the previous paragraph—'in my name' (verse 37). Mark follows this with another saying which contains (in the Greek) the word 'name' (verse 41).

VARIOUS SAYINGS (verses 41–50)
(Matt. xviii. 6–14. Luke xvii. 1–2)

There seems to be little connection between the various statements here, except the recurrence of words which link together consecutive sayings. The word 'name' is found (in the Greek) in verse 41, as is brought out in R.S.V. (' ... because you bear the name of Christ'. The R.V. ['because ye are Christ's'] and N.E.B. ['because you are followers of the Messiah'] obscure this). So this saying is linked with verses 38 and 39. The saying in verse 42, with its mention of 'little ones', recalls the reference to children in verse 37, and is also placed next to verse 41 to show the contrasting actions. The link between verses 43–47 and verse 42 is the Greek verb translated 'cause to stumble'; the phrase means literally 'scandalise' or 'trip up' (N.E.B. 'is your undoing; leads you astray'). Verse 48, with its mention of fire, leads on to verse 49, where the word is used in a different way, and the reference to salt leads on to verse 50a, and so on to the final statement in verse 50b, where the injunction 'Be at peace with one another' concludes the passage, apparently referring back to the dispute mentioned in verse 34. So the whole section consists of a somewhat artificial collection of sayings. They may have been already arranged in this way before Mark reproduced them in his book, as an aid to memory when converts were being instructed about the teaching of Jesus.

The millstone (verse 42) was a big stone used for grinding corn, which required an ass to turn it, in contrast to the hand-mill which a woman could use.

The Romans used to punish criminals by drowning in this way. The expression is figurative for utter destruction. The word translated 'hell' (verse 43) is Gehenna. This was the valley of Hinnom, a ravine south-west of Jerusalem. Sacrifices had been made here in Old Testament times to the pagan god Moloch. In the first century it was used as a dumping-ground for refuse from the city and fires were continually burning there to dispose of the rubbish. Hence the word Gehenna came to be used to denote a place of punishment for the wicked. The references here to 'fires which are not quenched and worms which do not die' (verse 48) are obviously metaphorical, standing for destruction. But 'fire' in verse 49 is the instrument of testing, not of destruction. Mark's readers would appreciate this in the light of the persecution which they themselves were undergoing. Salt (verse 50) cannot really become tasteless or 'lose its saltness', but if it is too much mixed with other ingredients it might lose its essential flavour or preserving power.

CHAPTER X

THE JOURNEY TOWARDS JERUSALEM

Teaching About Divorce (verses 1–12)
(Matt. xix. 1–12. Luke xvi. 18)

Jesus went to Perea and was asked about the Jewish law of divorce. In reply he laid down principles for marriage.

Galilee is not mentioned again in Mark, for Jesus now left that district and proceeded south. Mark devotes this one chapter to this journey towards Jerusalem. There is a further indication of its progress in verse 32. The company then arrive at Jericho (verse 46) and at the beginning of chapter xi they are approaching Jerusalem. The district described as 'beyond Jordan' (verse 1: N.E.B.: Transjordan) was Perea, east of the Jordan and the Dead Sea. Jews often went that way when travelling from Galilee to Jerusalem, to avoid going through Samaria, although that would be the most direct route. It is not certain whether Mark is describing a swift journey through Perea or a teaching ministry there of some duration.

The question put to Jesus, whether it was right for a man to divorce his wife (verse 2), was apparently an attempt to involve him in an argument. The Jewish Law certainly allowed this, recognising only the husband's right to divorce his wife; the woman had no such rights. The question which was debated in the rabbinic schools, which the Pharisees may have had in mind here, was the grounds for such divorce action. The followers of the rabbi Hillel allowed divorce for a number of causes, some of them quite trivial. The school of Shammai permitted it only for adultery. It is probable that Jesus was asked to give his judgment on these two rival opinions. The passage referred to in verse 4 about the regulations laid down by Moses (whose name was equivalent to the Law) is Deut. xxiv. 1, which stated that the wife was entitled to a legal document as evidence that her husband had divorced her.

Jesus did not answer directly the enquiry which had been put to him and apparently refused to be drawn into the current dispute. He said instead that divorce, although allowed by the Law, was a concession to the weakness of human nature. He then went back to the purpose of marriage, according to the Old Testament account, to show that it was a true union (verse 7); husband and wife therefore must not be separated by man (verse 9). It is noteworthy that Jesus' answer seems to put man and woman on an equal footing. The quotations in verses 6–7 are from Gen. i. 27 and ii. 24, from the Hebrew stories of the creation, and of Adam and Eve. As a Jew of the first century, Jesus shared the views of his contemporaries and apparently accepted these narratives as historical.

The explanation given to the disciples (verses 11–12) carries the argument a stage further. The words 'and marries another' are inserted, to show that what Jesus was forbidding or deprecating was a second marriage after divorce. Verse 12 is strange, for divorce by the wife was impossible under Jewish Law. (Some manuscripts have 'deserts her husband' instead of 'divorces her husband'.) Some think that this is an indirect

reference to the notorious case of Herodias, who
deserted her husband in order to marry Herod Antipas.

THE RECEPTION OF CHILDREN (verses 13–16)
(Matt. xix. 13–15. Luke xviii. 15–17)

*Jesus welcomed and blessed some children brought to him,
although the disciples wished to reject them, and added teaching
about receiving the kingdom of God as a child.*

The children were brought to be blessed by Jesus'
touch. Perhaps this was intended as a farewell, if he
had been for some time in the district. The disciples
rebuked those who brought the children, probably
because they wanted to save Jesus from trouble; they
did not think he wanted to be bothered. Jesus' answer
is in verse 14, and his action in verse 16 is the logical
consequence of this. But the saying about receiving
the kingdom of God (verse 15) breaks the connection
and would be more appropriate if attached to the
incident in ix. 33–35, where the disciples needed a
lesson on a child-like nature, after they had been
arguing about their own greatness. The statement there
(ix. 37) about receiving a child would be more fitting
in this narrative.

The saying here about accepting the kingdom 'like a
child' (verse 15) is ambiguous. It might mean 'as one
would receive a child' or 'as a child would receive the
kingdom'—simply and naturally; or it might be a
general statement that the kingdom belongs to people
like children, another version of the saying that people
must become like children in order to enter the kingdom (Matt. xviii. 3).

THE RICH MAN (verses 17–31)
(Matt. xix. 16–30. Luke xviii. 18–30)

A man wanted to know how to gain eternal life. Jesus told him
not only to keep the Law but to sell his possessions and follow
him, but he could not face the demand. Jesus then gave the
disciples teaching about the difficulty for the rich to attain
God's kingdom.

Matthew calls this enquirer a young man and Luke
terms him a 'ruler'. His statement in Mark (verse 20)
that he had observed the Law from his youth suggests
that he was no longer young. He asked Jesus about
eternal life (verse 17)—a term found in Mark only
twice, here and in x. 30. It seems clear from Jesus'
words in verses 23 and 25 that this meant the same as
the kingdom of God. He addressed Jesus as 'Good
teacher'; it is not necessary to suppose that this was
flattery. Jesus repudiated the title; his answer (verse
18) is an instance of his humility. Only God was good
and he did not wish to be put on a level with God; he
was drawing a contrast between the human goodness
which he shared and the divine, the only real goodness.

There are vivid touches in Mark's narrative—the
man came running to Jesus (verse 17), who 'looked
straight at him' (verse 21–N.E.B.) and 'loved him'
(N.E.B.: 'his heart warmed to him'). Jesus' command to
him to sell his possessions was intended only for this
man; there is no evidence that he required this of all
his followers. This man's wealth was a stumbling-block
to him, which he had to get rid of (cf. ix. 43ff.). Jesus
apparently failed with him, yet the Gospels reproduced
the story.

The incident is followed by a talk to the disciples

(verses 23–31) about the difficulty for rich men to attain the kingdom, and for others as well. In some manuscripts verses 24 and 25 are transposed. In this case Jesus first makes a statement about rich men (verse 23), which is elaborated in verse 25. He follows this up with a further remark that it is difficult for anyone at all to enter the kingdom (verse 24). It is this which causes astonishment among the disciples (verse 26). The statement about the camel and the needle's eye is an exaggeration—a deliberate hyperbole. The rabbis had a similar saying about an elephant. Various attempts have been made to explain it away—a popular one is that it referred to a gate in a city wall—but these are without foundation. It is simply an eastern way of saying 'It can't be done!' Jesus himself modified it when he added that with God all things were possible (verse 27)—even apparently for a rich man to enter the kingdom.

Peter, impetuous again, claimed that he and his fellow-disciples at any rate had fulfilled Jesus' requirements (verse 28). The rewards which Jesus held out in reply (verses 29–30) are not of course to be taken literally but indicate ample compensation for what has been given up. The words 'with persecutions' would have a special significance for Mark's readers.

THIRD STATEMENT OF THE PASSION (verses 32–34)
  (Matt. xx. 17–19. Luke xviii. 31–34)

Jesus again warned the disciples of the fate of the Son of Man at Jerusalem.

For the first time Jerusalem is mentioned as the goal of the journey. This prediction is much more detailed than the previous ones (viii. 31; ix. 31), including mention of condemnation by the priests, handing over to the Gentiles, mocking, spitting and scourging. The wording obviously owes much to the narrator's knowledge of the details of the trial of Jesus before the Sanhedrin and Pilate.

THE REQUEST OF JAMES AND JOHN (verses 35–45)
(Matt. xx. 20–28)

The sons of Zebedee demanded the chief places beside Jesus in glory. When the other disciples were indignqnt about this, Jesus told them that the truly great was not the one who ruled but the one who served.

This story is true to the character of the two brothers, as 'sons of thunder' (cf. ix. 38). In making their request they may have been thinking of the position of the chief officers of state sitting on either side of a king on his throne, or they may have had in mind the idea of the messianic banquet, a common figure of speech among the Jews, at which the chief guests reclined by the side of the host. Their demand shows that the disciples were still looking for a glorious and visible kingdom of the Messiah. In his answer Jesus referred to a 'cup' which they would have to drink and a 'baptism' they would have to undergo (verse 38). 'Cup' in the Old Testament is used, chiefly in the prophets, as a metaphor for suffering. 'Baptism' does not occur in this connection; it is here probably associated with the idea of calamity. As water flows over the one who is being baptised, so disaster flows over the sufferer. Jesus' words (verse 39) were fulfilled in the case of at least one of the brothers, for James was put to death by Herod Agrippa I (Acts xii. 1). The two brothers were here both promised the same fate. There was a somewhat obscure tradition in the early Church that John also was put to death.

The narrative continues with Jesus' words to the disciples in general. The rulers referred to (verse 42) are the Roman or other Gentile ones. Their attitude towards their subjects is well expressed by the words 'they lord it over them'; the 'great ones' are their subordinate officials, such as the members of the 'civil service' who had to keep the natives in order and collect taxes from them for a proconsul in a Roman province. The Greek word translated 'minister' in the R.V. (verse 43) should be 'household servant', while the word translated 'servant' (verse 44) should be 'slave' (as in N.E.B.).

The account concludes with a comment on the whole situation (verse 45). The thought of the Son of Man as coming not to be served but to serve is appropriate and enforces the teaching given in the preceding verses, but the words 'and to give his life as a ransom for many' do not follow logically either from this teaching or from the incident which started the discussion, where the thought is of service, not of sacrificing one's life. This final statement seems to incorporate the theological view of the death of Christ which was current in the Church when Mark wrote and is often considered as an addition and not the words of Jesus. It may have originated in the comment of a preacher as he concluded the narrative.

The word for 'ransom' meant originally the price paid for the redemption of a slave and was then used for a purchase price in general. Thus the word became associated with the thought of a deliverance which cost something. The use here is of course figurative and the metaphor must not be pressed; there is no suggestion of a payment being made to anybody. The thought behind the saying is that found in the Servant-poems of Deutero-Isaiah, where the death of the servant is said to benefit 'many' (Isa. liii. 11–12). The term Son of Man is again linked with the conception of service and sacrifice (cf. viii. 31).

THE HEALING OF BLIND BARTIMAEUS (verses 46–52)
   (Matt. xx. 29–34. Luke xviii. 35–43)

On reaching Jericho, Jesus was appealed to by a blind man begging, and hailed as Son of David. He called the man to him and, after asking him what he wanted, restored his sight.

Jericho, west of the Jordan and a few miles north of the Dead Sea, was the last town through which Jesus would pass on the way to Jerusalem. Then there was a road of sixteen miles to the capital. Pilgrims on the way there would gather at Jericho from different places.

This is, in Mark, Jesus' last act of healing. It was also the first time that he had been publicly called Son of David. The blind man, when he cried out this, was using a messianic title (verse 47), for the Jews hoped for a king who would restore the glories of David's line. Such would be a 'son of David', even if not actually descended from the royal line. Perhaps the blind man showed more insight into the office and character of Jesus, just as demented people had done, than others with full physical sight, but his cry may have been a mere conjecture on his part.

Jesus put to Bartimaeus what seems like a strange question—'What do you want me to do?' (verse 51). But this was in accord with his usual practice of getting a sufferer to make some kind of effort (cf. ii. 11; iii. 5). Here he wanted the blind man at least to express his need, before he healed him. In answer he addressed Jesus as 'Rabboni' (verse 51), a stronger form of the title Rabbi, 'my master'.

CHAPTER XI

JESUS IN JERUSALEM

THE ENTRY INTO THE CITY (verses 1–11)
  (Matt. xxi. 1-11.Luke xix. 28–44)

Approaching Jerusalem, Jesus sent two disciples to procure a colt. On this he rode into the city, accompanied by the acclamation of the crowd.

The site of Bethphage (verse 1) is uncertain, but Bethany was a village about a mile and a half east of Jerusalem, on the Jericho road. The words which Jesus instructed the disciples to repeat to anyone who asked them their business (verse 3) appear to be a kind of 'password' and it is generally assumed that he had made private arrangements for the colt to be ready. The 'lord' (or 'master') is generally taken to mean Jesus, who required the animal and promised to return it when he had finished with it. But the word might well refer to the owner of the colt (there is no word for 'our', which is inserted in N.E.B.); the disciples were to say to the bystanders that the owner had authorised them to fetch the animal.

The Greek word used for the animal on which Jesus rode meant the young of a horse or an ass. Jesus may have had in mind the only passage in the Old Testament where a king is said to come in peace (Zech. ix. 9). The word Hosanna (verse 9), which the people shouted, means in Hebrew 'Save us now'. They may have been calling upon Jesus to save the nation, perhaps to deliver them from the Romans, but Mark takes it as a cry of praise. It is a quotation from Ps. cxviii. 25-26, there the words should be translated: 'A blessing in the name of Yahweh on him who comes.' It was used to greet pilgrims as they approached the temple for the festival.

The ovation was probably made by Galilean pilgrims, for the inhabitants of Jerusalem would not have greeted a provincial prophet in this way. Jesus himself may not have wished for this kind of welcome. It is often assumed that Jesus by this act was claiming to be Messiah. But no such accusation was made against him at his trial before the Jewish authorities and Jesus himself made no attempt to follow up this welcome. He simply looked around the city and the Temple and returned to Bethany (verse 11). It is also doubtful if he would have played into his enemies' hands by openly making such a claim. He probably chose the colt as the animal used by ordinary travellers, to teach his disciples and his Galilean followers that he had come in peace and to discourage a messianic outburst.

THE UNFRUITFUL FIG-TREE (verses 12–14)
  (Matt. xxi. 18–19)

On seeing a fig-tree by the roadside without fruit on it, Jesus said that nobody would take fruit from it any more.

This narrative is continued in verses 20–25, which relate that by next morning the fig-tree had withered. It is uncertain what Jesus expected to find as he approached the tree. No figs were to be found on a tree at Passover time. Only green leaves appear in April–May, or some early green figs which are unpalatable. Mark

himself remarks that the time for figs had not yet come.
Another difficulty is the meaning of Jesus' words addressed to the tree (verse 14). They might be taken as
equivalent to a prohibition; Peter assumed that Jesus
had 'cursed' the tree (verse 21). They may, however, be
simply a statement of fact, about the future fate of the
tree. Perhaps the tree was already rotten and dying and
Jesus remarked that nobody would eat any more fruit
of it. The disciples heard it (as Mark seems to go out of
his way to mention) but apparently misunderstood
Jesus' meaning.

THE CLEARING OF THE TEMPLE COURT (verses 15-19)
   (Matt. xxi. 12-17. Luke xix. 45-48)

*Jesus entered the Temple court and ordered out those who were
changing money and selling doves. This action made the priests
determined to get rid of him.*

The part of the Temple into which Jesus entered was
the outer courtyard which ran all round the area, into
which people of any nation were admitted—the Court
of the Gentiles. In this there was a market which supplied pilgrims with materials for sacrifices: lambs (for
the Passover meal) and doves or pigeons, which were
given as offerings by poor people, and oil and wine.
Jews who had come from other countries were also
supplied here with the special money which the Jewish
authorities minted, with which a toll had to be paid
towards the upkeep of the Temple. Roman coins which
the visitors had brought with them were changed into
this. The money-changers made a profit, as did also
the priestly authorities who hired out the Temple court
for all this trading. It appears from the statement in
verse 16 that people were also in the habit of making a

short-cut through the Temple court, carrying goods from one part of the city to another.

Jesus was indignant at the sight and ordered the marketeers out. There is no suggestion of violence towards them. There was a Roman guard stationed in the Tower of Antony which overlooked the Temple area and these troops would have intervened if there had been any riotous action or display of force, as they did nearly thirty years later when Paul was assaulted (Acts xxi. 32). Once again Jesus seems to have made no attempt to take advantage of the popular enthusiasm which he may have aroused. He merely taught the people and went away (verses 18–19). But his action had brought against him some new enemies. This is the first time that priests have been mentioned as intent on doing away with him (verse 18).

When challenged about his action, Jesus quoted two passages from the Old Testament (verse 17)—Isa. lvi. 7 (the Temple as a house of prayer) and Jer. vii. 11 (the Temple as a den of robbers). Both prophets spoke of course about Solomon's Temple. Perhaps Jesus stressed the words 'for all the nations' in the quotation from Isaiah, being specially indignant that such practices were carried on in the court into which Gentiles were admitted—a bad example to other peoples of Jewish religious practices. In his words about the Temple Jeremiah was denouncing the people of his time who practised bloodshed and exploitation and then came to the Temple to make their sacrifices, turning it into a robbers' lair, a brigands' cave. Jesus felt that this was descriptive of the practices of the custodians of the Temple of his own day.

THE WITHERED FIG-TREE (verses 20–25)
(Matt. xxi. 20–22)

Next morning Peter called Jesus' attention to the state of the fig-tree, which had withered. Jesus then gave teaching about faith, prayer and forgiveness.

This is the continuation of the incident in verses 12–14. Peter assumed Jesus had cursed the tree because it did not bear any fruit. We cannot tell what Jesus' view of this was, for no answer of his to Peter's exclamation is reported. Instead, there are appended a number of sayings about faith and prayer.

This incident of the fig-tree has several puzzling features and various attempts have been made to deal with the questions that arise. Some have thought that Jesus was grieved at seeing no fruit on the tree with which he might satisfy his hunger and vented his anger by causing it to wither. But he knew, as Mark points out, that figs were not to be expected at that time. And moreover such an action—a miracle of destruction— would be a petulant one, quite unworthy of Jesus as he is portrayed in the Gospels. If this were all that there was in it, the occasion would surely not have been recorded. The writers of the Gospels were not concerned to relate mere 'wonders' without any moral or spiritual purpose. A more probable suggestion is that there was a fig-tree on the road between Bethany and Jerusalem which was already dead or withering. Jesus pointed out this to the disciples as they passed and likened it to the state of his nation and its religion. If Judaism was un-fruitful, it would wither as the tree had done. Its example was intended as a lesson for the disciples, but the story was later told as if Jesus had caused it himself.

There is a parable with something of the same lesson in Luke xiii. 6–9, where the fig-tree, threatened with destruction if it did not bear fruit, obviously stands for Judaism. It is possible that some such warning of Jesus was passed on in two forms. In Luke it was retained as a parable but it became 'hardened' into an incident in the form in which Mark heard it.

The sayings which follow (verses 22–25) have no connection with this incident. They were probably delivered on other occasions. 'Have faith in God' (verse 22) has no bearing on the example of the fig-tree. It is possible that there was a proverbial saying about 'faith that could remove mountains', which was known also to Paul (cf. 1 Cor. xiii. 2). The reference to 'this mountain' seems strange (verse 23), but it might refer to Mount Zion, on which the Temple stood—a hint that Jesus foresaw the end of the Temple system, as Judaism was superseded by the work of his disciples. There might thus have been some connection in Mark's mind between this statement and the warning about the fig-tree, if that stood for Judaism. The saying about prayer (verse 24) may have become attached to the preceding one by the recurrence of the word 'believe'. The only connection between verse 24 and verse 25 is the mention of praying. The arrangement of verses 23–25 is thus like that in Mark ix. 41–50, where isolated sayings are connected by the recurrence of key-words.

THE QUESTION OF JESUS' AUTHORITY (verses 27–33)
(Matt. xxi. 23–27. Luke xx. 1–8)

The religious leaders challenged Jesus in the Temple about his authority. In turn, he asked them whether John the baptist's work was of divine or human origin. When they were unable to answer him he refused to reply to their question.

This is the first of a series of challenges to Jesus in Jerusalem, continued in xii. 1–34. Just as Mark collected the conflict-stories from incidents in Galilee (ii–iii), so he now shows the opposition to Jesus in the capital city. But the grounds of the opposition are quite different, and it comes here mainly from the priestly and ruling classes. The priests, scribes and elders (verse 27) constituted the three classes of people in the Sanhedrin (cf. viii. 31). Those who brought this question to Jesus may have been a semi-official delegation from that body or merely members who happened to be present. They were quite within their rights in demanding what was Jesus' authority for teaching in the Temple court and especially for his action in ordering out those who had their permission to trade there.

The question was also probably somewhat of a trap, for whatever Jesus said the priests could have disputed it. So he refused to answer their question. Instead, as he often did, he gave the questioners the means of answering it themselves. The phrase 'the baptism of John' (verse 30) stands for his work as a whole—his call to repentance and his baptism of those who responded. The true prophet in the Old Testament was considered to have received his authority from God. The people regarded John as one such. The implication of Jesus' question was that they should accordingly likewise acknowledge him as a prophet. Since they could not make up their minds about John, he would give them no help in deciding his own credentials. It is characteristic of Mark's realistic style that he graphically breaks off the argument of the priests in the middle of a sentence, putting in his own comment (verse 32).

CHAPTER XII

CONTROVERSY IN JERUSALEM

THE PARABLE OF THE VINEYARD (verses 1–12)
(Matt. xxi. 33–46. Luke xx. 9–19)

*Jesus told a story about the tenants of a vineyard, who refused
to render their dues to the owner and ill-treated his servants and
killed his son. He declared that the men would be punished and
the vineyard given to others. The authorities sought to arrest
him, but did not dare to do so.*

The opening words of the parable recall Isa. v. 1ff., a
poem in which the prophet pictures a vineyard which
did not produce fruit and so was destroyed. Israel was
frequently spoken of in the Old Testament as Yahweh's
vineyard, which he tended and from which he expected
results. This parable seems to be thus in part allegorical,
although each detail must not be stressed. The preparations mentioned in verse 1, for instance, were the normal
ones for protecting a vineyard. A pit was dug under-
neath the press in which the grapes were squeezed, into
which the juice could fall. The hedge or wall was to
protect the vineyard from wild animals. The tower was
for a watchman, to look out for robbers. These details
are merely the background of the story and have no
special significance. The owner, however, seems plainly
to represent God, who had prepared the vineyard. The
servants sent to collect the fruit—the share of the
produce to which the owner was entitled—would be

prophets and other messengers of God. After they had been badly treated the son of the owner was sent, whom they killed. Jesus' hearers would probably understand this to refer to the Messiah. Jesus was showing that the Jews, not necessarily only those of his own time, had proved unfaithful in the trust reposed in them.

The parable as told by Jesus may have finished at verse 8, with the rejection and killing of the son. The question which follows: 'What will the owner do?', and the answer, that he will destroy the tenants and give others the right of looking after the vineyard, are generally taken as stated by Jesus, but they might both be the comment of a narrator. If the words are from Jesus, he was announcing that the time of judgment on Israel was at hand. There is evidence elsewhere in the Gospels that Jesus foresaw the fate in store for the nation and warned about it (e.g. Mark xiii. 2). Forty years later indeed it was destroyed, when the Romans crushed the revolt of the Jews. The quotation in verses 10–11 is from Ps. cxviii. 22–23. The words may have related to the writer, despised by his enemies, or they may have referred to Israel, scorned by the nations but given a place of importance by God. The metaphor is taken from building operations. A stone cast aside as worthless is nevertheless found useful for a corner stone, at the junction of two walls, or as the keystone of an arch. Early Christians took the stone to mean the Messiah and the passage was often applied to Jesus, who was rejected by the Jewish leaders but raised to a place of supreme importance. It is quoted in this way in Acts iv. 11 and 1 Pet. ii. 7. The quotation here was probably added by a narrator, who wanted to add a 'proof text' to Jesus' parable. Mark comments that the Jews saw that the parable was directed against them; the leaders of the nation were incensed at the suggestion that they would reject the Messiah if he should be sent to them. Once again (as in xi. 18) they sought to do away with Jesus because he had attacked their privileges.

THE QUESTION OF TRIBUTE TO THE ROMANS (verses 13-17)
(Matt. xxii. 15-22. Luke xx. 20-26)

Pharisees and Herodians asked Jesus if the Jews should pay the taxes demanded by their Roman overlords. Jesus got them to acknowledge that they were using Caesar's money and showed where men's duties lay towards the State and towards God.

The Herodians are mentioned only here and in iii. 6, both times associated with the Pharisees, with whom normally they would have had little in common, especially in a political question such as the one they put to Jesus. The Pharisees were opposed to Roman rule in principle, holding it a shameful thing that they should be ruled by pagans. But they would not revolt, for their principle was that God was in charge of history and it was not man's place to force his hand. The Herodians, however, would probably give their general support to the Romans, since they kept the Herods in power. The two parties thought that they had caught Jesus with their question, whatever answer he gave. If he said 'Yes, pay your taxes', he would have lost his popularity with the people and offended the Pharisees. If he said 'No', he would be uttering treason against Rome and offending the Herodians.

The Romans had levied a tax on the population of Judea from A.D. 6, when it became part of a Roman province, under a procurator. The tax was a denarius a head—a silver piece. Judas of Galilee had revolted against the census which had been taken as a preliminary to the imposition of the tax, which had to be paid in Roman coins, with the head and inscription of the emperor on them. The contemporary idea was that a coin belonged to the ruler whose inscription it bore and his authority was considered to hold as far as his coins circulated. The point of Jesus' question (verse 16) and his final answer was that the Jews, by having such coins in their possession, acknowledged the Romans as their overlords. His reply recognised civil allegiance and its obligations. But, he implied, these must not usurp the allegiance due to God. It was a principle to be applied when the claims of the State and of God are in question. He did not define where one sphere ended and the other began but left it for the sincere enquirer to think out for himself.

A QUESTION ABOUT RESURRECTION (verses 18–27)
(Matt. xxii. 23–33. Luke xx. 27–40)

Sadducees asked Jesus about the situation in the resurrection of a woman who had married seven brothers. In his replies Jesus said that the resurrection state was not like earthly conditions and argued from the Old Testament for a continuance of life after death.

The Sadducees are mentioned here for the first time in Mark. They were a small select body of Jews, many of whom held high office in Church and State and were aristocrats or priests. The party arose in the second century B.C., about the time of the origin of the Pharisees, when the Jewish nation was split on the question of their attitude towards foreign culture. The Sadducees were prepared to compromise with Greek ideas and practices. As Jews, they accepted the written Law—the

first five books of the Old Testament—as authoritative
but rejected all else, such as the oral traditions accepted
by the Pharisees. They consequently refused to accept
belief in a resurrection and future rewards and punish-
ments. These ideas are spoken of in only a few late
passages in the Old Testament, where the usual conception of the state of men after death was of a shadowy
existence in Sheol, the underworld (the Greek Hades).
The hope of a return from Sheol for judgment by God
developed probably under the influence of Persian
religion. In the second century B.C. the idea gained
strength under the stress of persecution, and the resurrection came to be regarded as a vindication of the
faithful who had suffered under heathen oppressors. By
the time of Jesus the idea was generally accepted by
Jews but there was no agreed conception of the resurrection state. Some crudely thought of a return to this
earth with the same body, while others favoured a
spiritual body. The subject of resurrection was a bone of
contention between Sadducees and Pharisees.

The Sadducees apparently assumed that Jesus upheld
the belief in a resurrection. The question they asked was
probably a standard catch which they were accustomed
to put to Pharisees. The law which they quoted (verse
19) (ascribing it to Moses, which was the usual conven-
tion) is in Deut. xxv. 5–6. The purpose of this regulation
was to maintain family inheritance and the rights of
property. It is uncertain how far it was practised in
Jesus' time and in any case the instance given by the
Sadducees was an extreme and absurd one. They perhaps wished to make Jesus appear foolish.

In reply Jesus first gave them a general rebuke (verse
24) and followed this with two separate answers. The
first was that earthly conditions do not continue in a

resurrection state (verse 25). (Jesus did not say that men and women became angels but were 'like angels', in that they did not marry.) This shows a more spiritual idea of resurrection than was implied in many Jewish beliefs of that time. His second answer (verses 26–27) was based on a passage from Exod. iii. 6—part of the Old Testament accepted by the Sadducees themselves. The words were spoken to Moses when he saw the burning bush and received his commission to deliver the Hebrews from Egypt. The statement meant that the speaker, Yahweh, was the God worshipped by Abraham, Isaac and Jacob, the early Hebrew patriarchs, to show Moses who it was who was speaking. It did not necessarily mean that these men were still alive in the time of Moses and has no real bearing on the question of a resurrection or a future life. Jesus argued that since God spoke in this way there was still a relationship between the patriarchs and himself and, since he is not a God of dead men, they must even then have been living. The argument is rabbinic in nature, with more force for Jesus' contemporaries than for us.

Both Jesus' answers seem to argue for the continuance of life after death rather than for a resurrection, but perhaps he regarded the greater as including the less, for without survival there could obviously be no resurrection.

THE QUESTION OF THE FIRST COMMANDMENT (verses 28–34)

(Matt. xxii. 34–40)

A scribe asked Jesus which was the most important of the commandments. After Jesus had quoted the laws about the love of God and of one's neighbour and the scribe had concurred, Jesus said he was not far from the kingdom of God.

The scribes were the exponents of the Law (see note on i. 22) and sometimes discussed it among themselves, attempting to distinguish between the more and the less important commandments, although theoretically they were all supposed to be of equal value, since all were considered to be the words of God. It has been calculated that in the Old Testament there are 613 commandments—365 negative ones and 248 positive ones. The question of this scribe may have been an attempt to involve Jesus in such an argument, but it was quite possibly a genuine enquiry.

In his reply (verses 29–30) Jesus quoted first from Deut. vi. 4–5 a passage known as the *Shema* (from the opening Hebrew word, 'Hear'), which was repeated every day by Jews. Every Jew would agree that this was the greatest commandment and the foundation of their religion—that men must have one God and must love him with their whole personality (the meaning of heart, soul, mind and strength). Jesus' second quotation is from Lev. xix. 18. There 'neighbour' meant a fellow-Israelite, although no doubt Jesus would have included men of other races and nations as well. The scribe's comment (verse 33) summarises the view of many of the Old Testament prophets—that morality and the love of God are more valuable than sacrifice and ritual. Jesus' words of commendation, that the scribe was not far from the kingdom, are another indication that he thought of this as the rule of God to be established within men.

A QUESTION ABOUT DAVID'S SON (verses 35–37a)
 (Matt. xxii. 41–46. Luke xx. 41–44)

Jesus asked in what way the Messiah was the son of David, since David had spoken of him as his lord.

After the questions put to him, Jesus himself proposed one; this may be the only one preserved of a number which he put to the religious leaders. He referred to the popular idea that the Messiah would be a descendant of David (as Bartimaeus had acclaimed Jesus himself at Jericho—x. 47); like the hero-king, he would restore the national greatness. But, he asked, how could this be, since David himself had acknowledged him as his 'lord'? The arguments depended upon a quotation from Ps. cx. 1, which was not written by David but was addressed to a Jewish ruler who was both priest and king—probably Simon Maccabaeus, about 141 B.C. The verse meant: God (the Lord) said to the king (my lord): Sit here and I will subdue your enemies for you. Jesus assumed the psalm had been written by David; as a Jew of the first century he naturally shared the views of his contemporaries on historical and literary matters. The Jews considered the verse to mean that God was addressing the Messiah, whom David, the writer, called 'my lord'. How then, asked Jesus, could the Messiah be descended from David, if David acknowledged that he was superior to him?

No answer is given to Jesus' question and it is uncertain what his argument was intended to mean. Some think that he was declaring that the Messiah was not a descendant of David at all, or not necessarily so. But it is usually taken to mean that the Messiah was greater than a mere son of David. Jesus probably wanted his hearers to think out the meaning of messiahship for themselves, apart from the conventional view.

Warnings Against the Scribes (verses 37b–40)
(Matt. xxiii. Luke xx. 45–47)

Jesus warned people against the show, arrogance and injustice of the scribes or doctors of the Law.

This section bears no relation to the previous paragraph but there is a link in the mention of scribes in verse 35. Not all the scribes of course would come under this condemnation by Jesus; he had already said that one at least was 'not far from the kingdom of God'. The chief seats in the synagogues (verse 39) were those facing the congregation, before the cupboard which contained the rolls of the Old Testament books. The 'first [or best] seats' ('seats of honour'–N.E.B.) at feasts were those to the left and right of the host. The reference to widows' houses or property (verse 40) may mean that scribes acted unworthily as trustees for the estates of widows. In the East the widow is representative of those with nobody to support or champion them.

The Widow's Mites (verses 41–44)
(Luke xxi. 1–4)

Jesus drew the attention of the disciples to a widow who had put two small coins into the treasury and declared that she had put in more than the rich people.

Once again Mark links a paragraph on to the preceding one by the repetition of a word or phrase ('widows' in verse 40). The treasury (verse 41) was in the Court of the Women, through which one had to pass in order to reach the Court of the Men of Israel. A priest sat nearby and the amount of each offering had to be declared to him. The coins which the woman put in were two *lepta*—brass coins—which made a Roman *quadrans*. Mark's Roman readers would appreciate the paucity of her gift and the poverty of the woman, yet she had put in all her income, whereas the others had given what they could well afford.

CHAPTER XIII

APOCALYPTIC TEACHING

THIS chapter is unique in Mark, consisting of a long discourse of Jesus, delivered on one occasion. It is introduced by the question of some disciples about the destruction of the Temple, and goes on to speak of signs of the end of the age and the coming of the Son of Man. Much of the material here is found also in writings of the centuries immediately before and after the time of Jesus—the apocalyptic literature. The Greek word 'apocalypse' means unveiling, the Latin equivalent of which gives us 'revelation'. It signifies the disclosure to men of events in the future, beyond human knowledge, revealed by God. The authors of these books sought to make known to their readers the revelation which had been granted to them and they often wrote in cryptic form, using symbolic and pictorial language; they showed that the evils of the present time would lead to a climax of wickedness, which would be followed by the victory of God's cause. These books were generally produced in times of oppression or persecution, to encourage those whose faith was being tested. In the Old Testament this type of literature is represented by Joel and Daniel and passages in some other prophetic books, and in the New Testament by the book of Revelation.

The early Christians inherited the Jewish apocalyptic outlook to a large extent and many of them, living in expectation of the return of Christ and the end of the age, compiled apocalypses which followed the main lines of the Jewish pattern but had in addition a Christian note. Mark xiii has much of this atmosphere. The conventional apocalyptic 'signs' are detailed—wars, revolts, famines, desecration, tribulation, wonders in the sky, culminating in the appearance of the Son of Man. This seems foreign to the outlook of Jesus, for he deprecated the search for such 'signs' and refused to give one (Mark viii. 12; cf. Luke xvii. 20–21) and spoke of the Son of Man as one who suffered and served; his conception of the kingdom of God was different from the wild speculations of the apocalyptists. It has consequently been suggested that in Mark xiii there have been included, together with some teaching of Jesus, extracts from a Christian apocalyptic writing. This document (generally called the Little Apocalypse) appears to have been used in verses 7–8, 14–20 and 24–27, for these passages contain typical apocalyptic ideas and language. Even if we consider that Mark did not use such a definite written source, yet it is clear that he employed in these places much of the conventional apocalyptic to expand the teaching of Jesus. Much of the chapter clearly does consist of genuine sayings of Jesus—warnings to the disciples about persecution (verses 9–13), about misleading claimants (verses 21–23) and exhortations to watch and be on the alert (verses 28–37), parallels to which are found in other places in the Gospels.

The whole chapter is set out as an apocalyptic discourse delivered to four chosen disciples. It was intended as a message to Mark's readers. He wished to assure the Christians, who were persecuted and perhaps wondered why Jesus did not come to save them, that their expectation of an early return of Christ was mistaken, that the apocalyptic 'signs' would have to appear first, that the Son of Man would eventually come, but Jesus had warned his followers in advance about their trials and had assured them that he would see them through.

THE COMING DESTRUCTION OF THE TEMPLE (verses 1–4)
(Matt. xxiv. 1–3. Luke xxi. 5–7)

Jesus told his disciples that the Temple would be utterly destroyed. Four disciples asked him when this would happen.

The Temple was started under the direction of Herod the Great in 20 B.C. and was still unfinished. The whole area was of great size and magnificence. The Temple building was of white marble and the front was covered with gold plates. It was destroyed by the Romans in A.D. 70. With his knowledge of the feelings of his fellow-Jews and his insight into the contemporary situation, Jesus could see the ultimate issue of the uneasy relations between the nation and the Romans. Old Testament prophets such as Jeremiah had in a similar way foreseen the end of Solomon's Temple at the hands of the Babylonians.

Peter, James and John, who had been picked out by Jesus on two previous occasions (v. 37; ix. 2) are here joined by Andrew. Their question (verse 4) does not receive an immediate reply. Possibly Jesus' answer is to be found in verse 30 ('It will take place in this generation'—that is, within thirty or forty years) or in verse 32 ('Nobody knows except God'). Mark uses their question as an introduction to apocalyptic teaching in general.

SIGNS OF THE END (verses 5–13)
    (Matt. xxiv. 4–14. Luke xxi. 8–19)

The disciples were told to take note of false claimants, wars, famines and disasters. They would be tried before the authorities and there would be family strife.

All the signs mentioned here (verses 7–8 and 12) were common features in apocalyptic speculations. When Mark wrote, there had been revolts in parts of the Roman empire and also famine and earthquakes, and he assured his readers that these were only 'the beginnings of travail'. The tribulations in which evil would grow stronger were thought of as the pains which would bring forth the Messiah—'the birth pangs of the new age' (verse 8–N.E.B.).

The warnings to the disciples in verses 9–13 were perhaps given on a number of occasions but were particularly appropriate just before the Passion. The wording was probably influenced by the experiences familiar to Mark and his readers. Some of them may have been brought before the Roman authorities and they would think of the trials of missionaries such as Paul. The word translated 'councils' or 'courts' (verse 9) is literally Sanhedrins. These were Jewish local courts of justice. Local synagogues performed a similar function; they had the right to try offenders against the Jewish Law and to punish them.

The statement in verse 10 about the universal preaching of the Gospel interrupts the sequence between verses 9 and 11 and is generally regarded as an insertion by Mark. He thereby assured his readers that in spite of persecution they must continue their mission. Jesus told the disciples that they would be helped by the Spirit (verse 11). This did not of course mean that every word of theirs would be dictated to them but that they would be encouraged to speak boldly and would be upheld. Many of the early disciples were uneducated men who might be overawed by the courts before which they had to defend themselves.

THE HORROR TO COME (verses 14–20)
(Matt. xxiv. 15–22. Luke xxi. 20–24)

The tribulation would reach its climax and men were then to take refuge and flee. But it would be cut short by God.

In the apocalyptic expectation the conflict between good and evil would culminate in the manifestation of an evil power. This was often regarded as personal—an anti-Christ, one who represented all that the Messiah was not. 'The abomination of desolation' (verse 14– R.V. and N.E.B.) is a Greek phrase which means 'an appalling horror which produces desolation' (R.S.V.: 'the desolating sacrilege'). The words are quoted from Dan. xi. 31 and xii. 11. They occur also in 1 Macc. i. 54, and refer to an altar to Zeus which was set up in the Temple court by the king Antiochus Epiphanes of Damascus, who had made Palestine part of his empire and was seeking to enforce Greek practices and religion on the Jews. The book of Daniel was written at that time. The crowning horror was the offering of swine's flesh upon this altar. The phrase is here made to refer to some horror similar to this, but in the future. Some have thought that Mark had in mind the attempt of the Roman emperor Caligula in A.D. 40 to set up his statue in the Temple court. This profanation did not actually take place, however, for news of his death arrived before the Roman governor could carry out his orders. It is more probable that Mark intended to refer to the presence of Roman armies and their standards in the city and the Temple area in A.D. 70. A difficulty is that the word 'abomination' (which is neuter in Greek) is followed by a participle in the masculine ('standing where he ought not'–R.V.; 'usurping a place which is not his'–N.E.B.). This may indicate that a personal figure was in mind—the anti-Christ or perhaps the Roman emperor who was behind the movement of his armies. If Mark wrote while the war was still going on, he could foresee the end—the occupation of Jerusalem by the Romans—but used vague language to forewarn his readers of this. The warnings in verses 15–16 do indeed reflect conditions in wartime, in face of an approaching enemy. The roof of a house was flat, and on it the occupant happened to be working or resting. He was to escape at once, by a stairway outside. If he was working on the land, he was to flee without returning home to fetch anything.

The parenthesis in verse 14—'let the reader understand'—is generally taken to mean that the reader of Daniel must note this new application of the passage about the abomination of desolation, or that the reader of the Little Apocalypse is warned to take special note. Possibly, however, the words were a note put by a scribe in an early copy of the Gospel, calling the attention of the man who read the book aloud in the Christian meeting to note that the masculine participle followed the neuter noun. A grammatical footnote thus became incorporated into the text.

Verses 19–20 return to the general idea of distress, a note on the dire nature of the tribulation. It was a common Jewish idea that this would last only for a limited period, otherwise everything good would be destroyed. For the sake of the 'elect'—those chosen by God to survive—it would have to be shortened. This originally meant the faithful Jews; the Christians took the phrase to relate to them.

WARNINGS AGAINST FALSE MESSIAHS (verses 21–23)
(Matt. xxiv. 23–28)

The disciples were not to be led astray by people claiming to be the Christ or prophets; they would deceive people.

This resumes the theme of verses 5–6. It was a current idea that the appearance of false teachers and deceivers would herald the conflict between good and evil. Jesus had probably warned his disciples that people might try to lead them astray, but the language here reflects rather the outlook of the early Church, who thought of themselves as the 'elect'. Verse 23 shows that no long-term prophecy is intended; the events foretold were expected to happen in the near future, to be witnessed by the disciples, or the readers of the Gospel.

THE APPEARANCE OF THE SON OF MAN (verses 24–27)
(Matt. xxiv. 29–31. Luke xxi. 25–28)

After unnatural phenomena in the sky, affecting the sun, moon and stars, the Son of Man would appear in the clouds and gather the chosen ones together.

This section is full of conventional apocalyptic matter and almost every phrase is a quotation from the Old Testament. The apocalyptists thought that the triumph of God would be preceded by disorders among the heavenly bodies (verses 24–25). A passage with a similar idea was quoted on the day of Pentecost by Peter (Acts ii. 20), who claimed that the prediction was being fulfilled that day! This is a warning against taking such speculations too literally. The reference to the appearance of the Son of Man (verse 26) recalls Dan. vii. 13–14 (see pp. 27 f.).

The Jews hoped that those of their nation who were dispersed among the Gentiles would return to Palestine for the final establishment of God's kingdom on earth; this was the 'gathering of the elect' (verse 27). For Mark's readers the phrase would mean the Christians throughout the world, who were to be brought together by the Son of Man. There is no indication here where this was supposed to happen, whether it was in the 'air' (as Paul imagined—1 Thess. iv. 17) or on the earth. The account breaks off suddenly; this bears out the suggestion that this section (verses 24–27) is part of the apocalypse which has been incorporated here.

THE PARABLE OF THE FIG-TREE (verses 28–32)
    (Matt. xxiv. 32–36. Luke xxi. 29–36)

Just as men can tell the season by noticing fruit on a tree, so the disciples were to observe these events, which would happen in their own time.

Jesus drew a comparison between the way in which men learn from observation of nature and the way they should know from these 'signs' that 'he is nigh' (verse 29–R.V.). But this should probably be 'it [i.e. the end] is near' (as N.E.B.). It is uncertain to what 'all this' refers, for it was to happen before that generation had died out (verse 30). Quite possibly this statement refers to the destruction of Jerusalem and the Temple and was the answer which Jesus gave to the question by the disciples with which the account opened (verse 4). In any case, the words in verse 30 show that Mark did not intend the predictions to be a long-term prophecy of events in the distant future. It is futile to attempt to find 'fulfilments' in the events of subsequent centuries or in modern times.

The statement that nobody knows the time of 'that day' or 'that hour' except God (verse 32) seems to contradict the statement in verse 30. A further difficulty is that it is the only place in Mark where the term 'the Son' by itself appears. It is generally assumed that Jesus was referring to himself and was confessing ignorance. But it might well be a comment by Mark, to deter speculation on the part of his readers. Alternatively, the wording may have been originally 'neither the son of man', meaning man; Jesus was saying that angels and men alike were ignorant of the future, which was known only to God.

The Parable of the Returning Householder (verses 33-37)
(Matt. xxiv. 42-51)

The disciples were to be on the alert, like servants waiting for the return of their master.

In this final paragraph, watchfulness is enjoined on the disciples. The statement that they did not know the time of the event, whatever it was (verses 33, 35), is inconsistent with the detailed 'signs' which had been given earlier in the chapter. It corresponds rather with teaching elsewhere, that the 'day of the Son of Man' would come suddenly, without warning (Luke xvii. 24). The concluding injunction to 'all' to watch (verse 37) is intended by Mark to extend Jesus' warning to the whole Church, and brings the discourse to a close.

CHAPTER XIV

THE TRIUMPH OF JESUS' ENEMIES

THE CONSPIRACY OF THE PRIESTS (verses 1–2)
(Matt. xxvi. 1–5. Luke xxii. 1–2)

As the Passover was near, the priests decided to arrest Jesus.

Mark gives, in the opening sentence here, the only statement in his Gospel of a definite date. The Passover was (and still is) one of the greatest feasts of the Jewish year. It was held in the spring (it occasionally coincides with our Easter) and originated in Old Testament times, commemorating the exodus from Egypt under Moses. The feast of unleavened bread, although originally separate, was associated with the Passover. It was observed for a week, beginning on the fifteenth day of the month Nisan of the Jewish year. No leaven (or yeast) was used in making bread during this week; this symbolised a break with the past and a fresh start.

For the third time Mark mentions the intention of the priests and scribes to arrest Jesus (xi. 18; xii. 12). Jesus' enemies were now these authorities of the Church and State. There is no mention of Pharisees, as in Galilee. It was the priests who carried through his arrest and trial and brought him before Pilate and stirred up the people to clamour for his death. The meaning of their statement here (verse 2) is uncertain. It is generally taken to indicate that they intended to arrest Jesus before the feast started, before there was a chance for a riot to develop in his favour. But the crowds had already assembled for the feast. So it might mean that they intended to leave him for a time and arrest him after the feast, when the pilgrims would have gone back to their homes. The Greek phrase could however be translated 'not among the festival crowd'— the priests sought a way to arrest Jesus when he was alone, away from the crowds with whom he was popular. This was what they eventually did.

THE ANOINTING OF JESUS AT BETHANY (verses 3–9) (Matt. xxvi. 6–13)

While Jesus was at a meal a woman anointed his head. Some protested at her action but Jesus defended her.

Bethany was the place from which Jesus had started his ride into Jerusalem (xi. 1). His host is called Simon the leper; he had presumably been cured of his leprosy (a term used for a number of skin diseases)—not necessarily by Jesus. The woman who anointed Jesus is unnamed and there is no ground for identifying her with any other woman mentioned in the Gospels. She was probably one of the guests. In the East the anointing of the head was a sign of special honour and was also the method used in consecrating kings and priests. The word Messiah means 'anointed' and possibly the woman was proclaiming her conviction that Jesus was this. The ointment or oil was contained in a phial made of alabaster (verse 3), which she would break by snapping off the neck. The word 'spikenard' (R.V.) probably means pure or genuine nard (R.S.V., N.E.B.). Its cost was estimated at 300 denarii (N.E.B.: thirty pounds)—a whole year's wages for a working man. The woman must have been wealthy to be able to afford this, although those who complained may have exaggerated the price. It is not clear who these people were—presumably fellow-diners, not necessarily Jesus' own disciples.

Jesus' reply (verse 8) was startling. He had just been treated as a person of honour and now started talking about being buried! Bodies were usually anointed after death; Jesus said that the woman had anticipated this. It was probably Mark (or a narrator before him) who added the final comment, that the story would be told wherever the Gospel was preached (verse 9), for he knew that by his time the Christian message was being proclaimed throughout the Roman world.

THE TREACHERY OF JUDAS (verses 10–11)
    (Matt. xxvi. 14–16. Luke xxi. 3–6)

Judas went to the priests and offered to deliver Jesus to them. They promised him a reward.

Judas has not been mentioned since his appointment as one of the twelve in iii. 19. This paragraph is a continuation of verses 1–2. The intervention of Judas resolved the dilemma of the priests. Mark gives no reason for Judas' action. Various suggestions have been made—that he was a Zealot and disappointed with Jesus' peaceful preaching of the kingdom, or that he wished to force Jesus' hand and make him exhibit his powers by resisting arrest—but these are all conjecture. His motive does not appear to have been mercenary, for it was after he had made his offer that the priests promised him a reward. Probably Judas' motives were mixed. He may have been jealous of the attention which Jesus gave to other disciples such as Peter. If he was a southerner, he may have felt 'out of it' among the

Galileans and it may have been simply spite which prompted him to go to the priests. It is not clear what he intended to disclose to them. Some think that he gave them a hint about Jesus' messiahship, which led the high priest to challenge Jesus on this at his trial (Mark xiv. 61). Possibly he merely said he was able to lead them to a place where Jesus could be taken, away from the crowds.

THE LAST SUPPER (verses 12–25)
(Matt. xxvi. 17–29. Luke xxii. 7–38)

Jesus told two disciples to make preparations for the Passover meal. He warned the disciples about a traitor among them. Distributing bread and wine, he told them that they represented his body and blood of a covenant.

Mark has identified the first day of unleavened bread with the feast of the Passover (verse 1), but the week of unleavened bread actually started on the following day. The instructions which Jesus gave to the two disciples (verses 13–15), like those given when they fetched the colt (xi. 2ff.), suggest that he had friends in the city with whom he had made arrangements. The sight of a man carrying a water-pot would be unusual, for women generally went to the well for water. Perhaps the man was a slave or a member of the household. Jesus made this secret arrangement probably because he did not wish Judas to know where he was and inform the priests before he had had this last opportunity of fellowship with the disciples.

The central feature of the Passover celebrations was a family meal. Each family in Jerusalem bought a lamb, which was taken to the priests at the temple; there its throat was cut and the blood thrown before the altars in the Temple court. The meat was then taken home, roasted and eaten with wine and bitter herbs and un-leavened bread. This was intended to recall the bitter-ness the Hebrews had felt when leaving Egypt and the haste in which they had to prepare their departure. At this supper Jesus first gave a warning about a traitor among the twelve (verses 17–21). He could no doubt sense the attitude of Judas and perhaps his words were Jesus' last appeal to him. He indicated a traitor in quite general words and there is no suggestion that the others knew whom he meant. The words 'one who is dipping in the same dish' (verse 20) simply mean 'one present at this table'. The term Son of Man is again linked with the idea of the Servant of whom it was written that he would go the way of suffering.

At a Jewish meal the host used to start by breaking a loaf and handing it round, after pronouncing and giving thanks for it. The usual words were: 'Blessed art thou, O Lord our God, who bringest forth bread from the earth.' Jesus here acted as the host (verse 22), as he no doubt always did when he and the disciples ate together. The words which he added, 'This is my body', would mean, in Aramaic: 'This means (or represents) me.' The host also pronounced a thanksgiving over the cup; 'Blessed art thou for the fruit of the vine.' Jesus added that the wine represented his blood, using the word covenant (verse 24). This term meant a compact or treaty between two people or nations, and was used in the Old Testament especially of the relationship be-tween Yahweh and Israel. The Greek word was trans-lated in the Latin version of the Gospels by *testamentum*. The old covenant had been made at Sinai and was instituted with the blood of an animal, with which the people were sprinkled (Exod. xxiv. 8). Jesus spoke as though he were instituting another covenant of which his own blood was the sign. The idea of a new covenant —one written not on tablets of stone but on the hearts of men—was pictured by the prophet Jeremiah (Jer. xxxi. 31–34) and this was probably in Jesus' mind. The words 'for many' may recall (as in x. 45) the last of the Servant-songs, in which the suffering of the Servant of God was held to benefit many (Isa. liii. 11–12).

In distributing the bread and the wine in this way, Jesus was demonstrating what he wanted to teach the disciples, in much the same way as Old Testament prophets sometimes acted their message to impress it on their contemporaries. Jesus used this method when he took a child as an object lesson (ix. 36) and when he entered Jerusalem (xi. 7). He was here giving a warning to his disciples that his body would be broken and his blood would be shed, like the bread which he had broken and the wine he had poured out at the table.

Finally, he told them that this was the last meal they would take together. Their table-fellowship would be resumed in the kingdom of God (verse 25). This reflects the Jewish idea of a messianic banquet, frequently used as an image of the kingdom.

JESUS AND THE DISCIPLES AT THE MOUNT OF OLIVES (verses 26–42)
(Matt. xxvi. 30–46. Luke xxii. 39–46)

They left the upper room and Jesus told the disciples that they would all desert him and Peter would deny him. At Gethsemane he prayed for deliverance, while the disciples failed to watch.

The hymn sung (verse 26) would be from Psalms cxv–cxviii, which were recited during the Passover celebrations. The quotation about the sheep and their shepherd (verse 27) is from Zech. xiii. 7, which Jesus evidently thought suited his situation. Peter's words of protest against this (verse 29) follow naturally, and the reference to a resurrection and meeting in Galilee (verse 28) breaks the sequence and seems out of place. It is difficult to see why the disciples were so discouraged and despairing after the crucifixion if Jesus had so recently spoken like this. The verse is probably an insertion by the narrator or Mark. In his warning to Peter (verse 30) Jesus probably told him he would deny him 'before cock-crow' (the word 'twice' is omitted in some manuscripts), meaning 'before dawn breaks'. The Romans divided the night into four watches and the beginning of the fourth watch (about 3 a.m.) was called 'cock-crow' (cf. xiii. 35).

The mount of Olives (verse 26) was situated east of Jerusalem, about a mile and a half from the city walls. Gethsemane (verse 32) is called in the Synoptics 'a piece of ground', not a garden. On the hillside there were orchards of olive-trees. Jesus again selected Peter, James and John (cf. v. 37; ix. 2; xiii. 3). Mark uses strong terms in speaking of Jesus' emotions—he was 'appalled, greatly astonished and in anguish' (verse 33). This suggests that Jesus had not anticipated that the result of his work and his appeal to his nation would be utter rejection and would result in the fate which he now saw before him. Perhaps he was also troubled at the disloyalty of his followers, as well as the treachery of Judas. Mark reproduces the Aramaic word for 'father', used by Jesus—*Abba*. His oft-quoted words after his prayer—'the spirit is willing but the flesh is weak'—are generally taken as his reflection on the conduct of his disciples, who could not keep awake, but it is equally possible that Jesus was speaking of himself and the inner conflict which was shown in his prayer. 'Flesh' means human nature on its earthly and weak side; 'spirit' means its higher aspirations. His final words to the disciples (verse 41) are probably a question: 'Still sleeping? Still taking your ease?' (N.E.B.)

THE ARREST OF JESUS (verses 43–52)
Matt. xxvi. 47–56. Luke xxii. 47–53)

An armed company from the priests seized Jesus when he was pointed out by Judas. He protested that they were treating him like a robber. The disciples deserted him.

The people who came to arrest Jesus were probably members of the Temple police—a guard of Levites who kept order in the courts, under the direction of the priests. Some, however, think that they were simply a mob collected for the purpose by the authorities. Judas' action in kissing Jesus was that of the disciple of a rabbi, who used to greet his master in this way (verse 45). Some such indication would be necessary in the dim light, even under the full moon of the Passover season. Jesus protested that they were treating him as if he were a brigand, who would resist arrest by force. The words added to this—'let the scriptures be fulfilled' (verse 49)—are probably a narrator's comment; they seem quite out of place on the lips of Jesus at this point.

All that the disciples could do, in spite of their recent protestations of loyalty, was to run away. Two other men, both of them unnamed, figure in Mark's account. One was the man who attempted to protect Jesus (verse 47). Mark calls him one of the bystanders, as if his presence there was almost accidental. If he had been one of the twelve, Mark would surely have named him, especially if he had been Peter. The high priest's slave whose ear was cut was possibly the man in charge of the party. The other unknown figure is the young man whose garment was taken from him (verses 51–52). It has been conjectured that it was the writer of the Gospel. It may have been an unknown disciple or someone who was present accidentally. Perhaps it was the person from whom Mark obtained his information about the scene in Gethsemane, who had overheard Jesus' prayer; none of the disciples could have reported this, for they had been asleep.

JESUS BEFORE THE HIGH PRIEST (verses 53–65)
(Matt. xxvi. 57–68. Luke xxii. 54–55, 63–71)

Before the Sanhedrin Jesus was accused of attacking the Temple. In reply to a question from the high priest he acknowledged that he was the Messiah and he was condemned for blasphemy. He was then subjected to mockery and abuse.

The high priest was Caiaphas, who held that office from A.D. 18 to 36, when he was removed by the Romans. His father-in-law, Annas, had been similarly deposed in A.D. 15. He was a Sadducee and presided over the Sanhedrin, which consisted of the 'priests, elders and scribes' ('doctors of the law'–N.E.B.) mentioned here. The name comes from a Greek word meaning a council and it constituted the governing body of the Jewish nation. There were seventy-one members in Jesus' time and it contained both Sadducees and Pharisees. It was the Roman practice to allow local or national courts of justice to function in provinces of the empire, and the Sanhedrin was authorised to try offenders against the Jewish religious and national laws.

Mark states that 'the whole council' were present (verse 55) but according to Jewish Law a full meeting of the Sanhedrin could not be held before dawn, so the assembly here described was illegal, unless it was merely an informal meeting of some members.

The proceedings suggest little knowledge of Jesus' teaching and activities, since they could not find grounds on which to accuse him (verse 55). According to Jewish Law, two witnesses had to be in agreement before a man could be tried on a capital charge (Deut. xix. 15; Num. xxxv. 30). The accusation made against Jesus was that he said he would destroy the Temple (verse 58). This may bear some relation to his words about the forthcoming destruction of the Temple and the city (xiii. 2). He had warned the Jews of the fate in store for the nation at the hands of the Romans and his words may have been twisted into a claim that he himself would effect its destruction. At the centre of Judaism was the sacrificial system, for which the Temple stood. So the accusation really meant: 'This man is attacking our religion.' This implied also an attack on the nation, since religion and politics were interwoven. Perhaps Jesus' enemies had realised what his own disciples apparently did not—that his spirit and teaching were incompatible with the continuance of the Jewish legal and sacrificial system.

The further statement attributed to Jesus, that he would within three days build an immaterial temple, probably referred to his teaching about the kingdom of God. It meant that the requirements of true worship could be satisfied without a material Temple and sacrifices. The term 'three days' is used in the Old Testament to indicate a short time, just as 'forty years' was a conventional phrase for a longer period.

Finally, since he could not get agreement among the witnesses, the high priest put to Jesus the question whether he was 'the Messiah, the Son of the Blessed' (verse 61). The Jews used such terms as 'the Blessed' or 'the Power' when speaking of God, to avoid using his name. The priest's action was illegal, for the judge was not allowed to challenge the prisoner into committing himself. A confession of messiahship might form the basis for a charge of blasphemy against God, although in itself such a claim did not constitute blasphemy. It could also be used as material for a charge of sedition against the Romans, since the Messiah was supposed to be of the royal line and the Romans did not allow anyone to call himself king without their permission. Jesus' answer was 'I am.' (This is the reading in most manuscripts, but some have: 'You say that I am'—i.e. 'The statement is yours.') This is the first time in Mark that Jesus claimed to be Messiah. Added to this reply are words taken from Dan. vii. 13, with phrases also from Ps. cx. 1. The passage in Daniel describes the writer's vision of 'one like a son of man' who approaches God and receives from him power and dominion. It has already been quoted in Mark xiii. 26. On the lips of Jesus here, it is often taken to refer to a 'second coming' of Christ, in glory, in contrast to the humble nature of his first coming. This interpretation overlooks the fact that there is nothing here, or in the Daniel passage, about a coming to the earth or to men; the 'figure like a man' in Daniel came to the Ancient of Days and was presented to him and received from him his power. This view would also mean that Jesus was mistaken in telling the members of the Sanhedrin this, for none of them witnessed any such event. It is more likely that it means that Jesus would be vindicated by God and his ultimate

triumph was assured, and the priests would realise this
—'*you* will see . . .'. But no disciple was present at the
meeting and only the vaguest reports would circulate
among the Christians later as to what took place; so
we cannot be sure that these were words of Jesus and
it is possible that they represent the comment of a
narrator or preacher by which he assured his hearers
that *they* would see the ultimate triumph of Jesus'
cause.

Jesus' answer made the high priest tear his robes—a
conventional sign of indignation and grief. Jesus was
condemned for blasphemy, the penalty for which was,
in Old Testament times at least, death by stoning (Lev.
xxiv. 16). The people who began to maltreat him (verse
65) were probably attendants, not members of the
Sanhedrin. They covered Jesus' eyes, so that he could
not see who his mockers were, and challenged him to
use the insight characteristic of a prophet to name his
assailants.

DENIALS BY PETER (verses 66–72)
  (Matt. xxvi. 69–75. Luke xxii. 56–62)

*When challenged by different people about his association with
Jesus, Peter denied it three times.*

The accounts in the Gospels do not agree who the
people were who challenged Peter. He himself would
probably be unable to remember exactly who had
spoken to him. Peter was first in the courtyard below
the room in which the trial was taking place. Afterwards
he went into the vestibule or porch leading from the
courtyard to the outer gate and thence into the street
(verse 68).

The last sentence of verse 72 is very obscure in the

Greek. It is literally: 'casting upon, he wept.' It was probably a current expression which meant 'he set to and wept.' The R.S.V. ('he broke down and wept') and Moffatt and N.E.B. ('he burst into tears') express the general meaning.

CHAPTER XV

THE TRIAL AND EXECUTION OF JESUS

THE TRIAL BEFORE PILATE (verses 1–20)
(Matt. xxvii. 1–31. Luke xxiii. 1–25)

Jesus was brought before the Roman governor and tried on a charge of being king of the Jews. The crowd shouted for the release of a rebel and for the crucifixion of Jesus. Pilate sent him for execution and the Roman soldiers indulged in mockery of him.

The 'whole council' which Mark says assembled at dawn may have been the official meeting of the Sanhedrin (verse 1), to pass sentence on Jesus and prepare their case for Pilate. The real trial then began. The Jews had the right to try a man on a religious charge but it is uncertain whether they were allowed to put a guilty man to death. Some Jewish rulers were evidently able to do this, for Herod Antipas had John the baptist beheaded (Mark vi. 27), Herod Agrippa had James killed (Acts xii. 1) and the Sanhedrin stoned Stephen (Acts vii. 58ff.). Some think that the Romans had taken this right away from the Jews, but in any case it would have been dangerous for them to have put Jesus to death at this time, as Pilate was in Jerusalem. Generally the procurator lived at Caesarea, on the Mediterranean coast, but he would have come to Jerusalem at Passover time to keep an eye on the festival crowds. He probably occupied the castle of Antony, a Roman fortress overlooking the Temple courts.

Judea had been under a Roman procurator since A.D. 6. In that year Herod Archelaus, one of the sons of Herod the Great, who ruled over the southern parts of Palestine, was deposed by the Romans and exiled. His subjects had appealed to Rome about his misgovernment of the territory. Judea (and Samaria) then came under direct Roman rule. Pontius Pilate was the fifth of the governors who had been appointed and held power from A.D. 26 to 36. He seems to have made little attempt to understand the Jews and was eventually recalled to Rome to answer charges of oppression, of which he was found guilty and banished from Italy. He is said by Philo, a Jewish writer of Alexandria (quoting Herod Agrippa I), to have been 'inflexible, merciless and obstinate', but in the accounts of the trial of Jesus he appears rather to be weak and vacillating; but we cannot rule out the possibility that the evangelists sought to put the chief blame for the crucifixion of Jesus upon the Jews and so glossed over Pilate's harsh treatment of him.

Mark does not state what accusations were made against Jesus here, but they evidently included a claim to be king of the Jews, for Pilate immediately asked Jesus about this (verse 2). This was a political matter; the charge of blasphemy was not mentioned, for this would have had no weight with a Roman governor. No ruler in the empire was allowed to use the title of king without being authorised by Rome. Jesus refused in effect to answer Pilate's question; his words mean 'That is your statement, not mine.' He knew that Pilate's idea of kingship was quite different from his.

Nothing is known of the custom of releasing a prisoner at a festival time (verse 6). Roman governors in other places occasionally used to release prisoners to the

populace and Pilate may have had this in mind. It is
unlikely that this was his general practice. Barabbas was
presumably a rebel against the Romans. The people
who clamoured for his release would not be the members of the Sanhedrin and were probably not the people
who had shouted 'Hosanna' on Jesus' entry into Jerusalem. Possibly some partisans of Barabbas arrived
during the trial, shouting for their hero to be released,
and Pilate, thinking he saw an opportunity to get rid of
this puzzling 'king of the Jews', offered them Jesus'
freedom instead, considering that the mob would be
satisfied if they had a self-styled king given to them. But
they seized the opportunity afforded by this display of
weakness on the part of Pilate and persisted in their
demand for Barabbas and now, urged on by the priests,
clamoured for the condemnation and execution of Jesus
(verse 11). After a vain attempt at justice (verse 14),
Pilate gave way.

Crucifixion was a Roman method of execution. The
responsibility was Pilate's. The usual preliminary to
crucifixion was a flogging on the bare back with a whip
or leather thongs loaded with bone or metal (verse 15).
The people who mocked Jesus (verse 16) would be the
Roman guard who were waiting while preparations for
the execution were being made. The purple cloak they
put on him would be in imitation of the robe worn by
the emperor, the crown of thorns would be a mocking
representation of the laurel wreath worn by victors at
the games; the emperor also wore a wreath on festal
occasions. 'Hail, king of the Jews' was a parody of the
salutation to the emperor: *Ave, Caesar*.

The Crucifixion (verses 21-32)
(Matt. xxvii. 32-44. Luke xxiii. 26-43)

Jesus' cross was carried by Simon to Golgotha and there he was crucified with two robbers. The people and the priests mocked him and challenged him to save himself.

After being flogged, the person condemned to crucifixion had to carry a heavy wooden bar—the crossbeam—to the place of execution. The upright stake was already in position in the ground. There he was nailed or bound to the cross-bar by his hands and was hauled up so that the beam fitted across the upright. His feet were generally tied, sometimes nailed, and were supported by a wooden ledge. There he was left to die, sometimes lasting for days, unless he was put out of his agony by the soldiers. The Romans considered crucifixion such a shameful form of punishment that they reserved it for slaves and subject-races, forbidding it to be used for Roman citizens.

Jesus apparently collapsed through exhaustion and Simon was impressed by the Romans into service, to carry the wood for him (verse 21). Cyrene was in Libya, in north Africa, and there was a Jewish colony there. Only Mark mentions the names of his sons, presumably because the men were known to his readers and had become Christians. The Romans had the right to force a bystander into such a service; there is no suggestion that Simon did this voluntarily. Golgotha (verse 22) may have been so called because the plot of ground was shaped like a skull or it may have been the site of a cemetery. None of the accounts says it was a hill, although this is quite possible. It was a Jewish practice to offer wine drugged with myrrh to a crucified

man, to dull his pain (verse 23). The Roman guard had
the right to the clothes of the criminal, who was crucified
naked, as some compensation for their weary task, for
they had to keep watch until the man died, so that his
friends might not rescue him (verse 24). The Romans
used to put an inscription over the head of the crucified
man, stating his crime (verse 26). The wording here
shows that it was on a political charge of claiming to be
king that Jesus was executed. For the Jews the words
would also suggest messiahship, hence their taunts
(verse 32).

The men crucified with Jesus were bandits or robbers.
It is unlikely that the people who passed along and
taunted Jesus actually included the chief priests, as
Mark says (verse 31), for they would have been about
their Passover duties. The people mentioned here may
have been their servants or simply those who shared
their views. The taunt about destroying the Temple
(verse 29b) recalls the accusation at the trial, except
that the statement that Jesus would erect another
Temple without hands was changed to the re-erection
of the same Temple—clearly an absurdity, perhaps
deliberate on their part.

THE DEATH OF JESUS (verses 33–41)
   (Matt. xxvii. 45–56. Luke xxiii. 44–49)

*After three hours of darkness, in the middle of the afternoon
Jesus cried out and died. The Roman centurion called him
God's son. Three women watched from a distance.*

The darkness 'over the whole land' (which probably
means Judea) could not have been caused by an
eclipse of the sun, as the moon is full at Passover time,
and an eclipse is impossible then. Some have suggested

that heavy clouds obscured the sun or that a storm arose from the south, which brought up sand from the desert. It is more probable that the 'darkness' should not be regarded as physical at all; it is a symbolic way of expressing the shadow which was over the land of the Jews at that time.

Mark gives Jesus' last words (verse 34) in Aramaic and translates them into Greek. The cry is a quotation from the opening words of Ps. xxii. The psalm is a description of the experiences of a righteous man in adversity. It seems to have been much in the mind of the writers of the Gospels as they told the story of the Passion, for there are echoes of its phrases in many places. Although it opens on what is apparently a cry of despair, it finishes on a note of triumph and confidence in God. Some have suggested that Jesus began to recite the whole psalm and only the opening words were heard. Others have thought that it does represent his real feelings at that time. His prayer in Gethsemane had apparently been unanswered. Men had failed to respond to his appeal and his preaching about God's reign. He had been betrayed by one of his followers and deserted by the rest. His life's work appeared to have been a failure and he could not but feel that he had been forsaken by God also.

The remark of the bystanders, who thought that he was calling upon Elijah (verse 35), reflects the popular idea that this prophet would come before the Messiah (cf. ix. 11) and also that he would come to the aid of those in need. It is difficult to see how Jews could have made such a remark, mistaking the word for God for the name of Elijah, unless they deliberately misunderstood Jesus and spoke in mockery. On the other hand, if the men who answered him were Romans, they would not know anything about Elijah. A Latin manuscript has, instead of Elijah (*Elias*), the word *helion* (the sun) and the suggestion has been made that they supposed that Jesus was appealing to the sun-god to help him through the darkness.

The vinegar or sour wine (verse 36) which was offered to Jesus, apparently out of compassion, was the drink of soldiers and working men. Mark adds a strange remark about the curtain in the Temple (verse 38). There were two such, one between the Holy Place and the Holy of Holies, in the innermost shrine, and the other between the Holy Place and the rest of the building. If either of these had been torn, only the priests would have known of it, for nobody else was allowed in there, and they would not have been likely to have told anyone. So Mark's statement is not to be taken literally; he wished to say that the death of Jesus meant the removal of the veil between God and man or the end of effective Judaism and the sacrificial system. The final remark was made by the centurion who was in charge of the execution squad (verse 39). There is no definite article in the Greek before the word 'son' and on his lips the words would mean: 'This was God's son' or perhaps 'This was a son of (a) God.' The Romans and Greeks had many stories about visits to earth by the gods and of semi-divine beings. But for Mark and his readers the term would mean the Messiah and the statement would recall the opening words of the book— 'The gospel of Jesus Christ, God's Son' (i. 1). The 'messianic secret' was out, proclaimed now by a Gentile.

Three women are named (verse 40) as watching with others at a distance; they would not be allowed near the crosses. Mary of Magdala came from a town in Galilee, on the western side of the lake. James the less (either in age or in stature), whose mother had the same name, was possibly the same man as James the son of Alphaeus, one of the twelve (iii. 18). Salome is not mentioned elsewhere in Mark. Apparently none of the men disciples witnessed the crucifixion.

THE ENTOMBMENT OF JESUS (verses 42–47)
(Matt. xxvii. 57–66. Luke xxiii. 50–56)

Joseph of Arimathaea asked Pilate for permission to take the body of Jesus. He wrapped it in linen and put it in a rock tomb.

Mark does not say that Joseph of Arimathaea (a town probably near Lydda in Judea, between Jerusalem and the coast) was a disciple of Jesus. The statement that he was 'looking for' (or 'eagerly awaiting'–N.E.B.) the kingdom of God (verse 43) may indicate no more than that he was a good and pious Jew, perhaps a Pharisee. As 'a member of the council' (by which Mark probably means the Sanhedrin) he may have desired to fulfil the Jewish Law that a body must not remain on the gallows all night, for that would defile the land, but must be buried the same day (Deut. xxi. 22–23). It would be a double disgrace for the body to stay there over the Passover Sabbath. So Joseph 'plucked up courage' (as Mark's words could well be translated) and, taking the risk of being identified with Jesus' followers, went to Pilate. He would have to get the help of other people to take the body down from the cross; he probably had servants whom he called upon to do this. Nothing further is told about Joseph in the New Testament; he is never mentioned in the Acts as being among the members of the early Church.

The Romans used to leave the body of a crucified

man on the cross unless some friends of his wanted to bury it and they were then allowed to remove it. In the case of Jesus this had to be done before sunset that day (Friday), as the Jewish Sabbath started then. After that, it would not be permitted to do this for twenty-four hours, for this constituted 'work'. The tomb (verse 46) into which the body was put would be a rock cavern, with a shelf on which a number of bodies could be laid. It was probably intended by Joseph as a temporary resting place until the Sabbath was over. He did not attend to the anointing of the body, which was usual among the Jews when a body was placed in such a tomb.

CHAPTER XVI

AFTER THE CRUCIFIXION

THE WOMEN'S VISIT TO THE TOMB (verses 1–8)
  (Matt. xxviii. 1–15. Luke xxiv. 1–12)

Two days afterwards, early in the morning, three women visited the tomb to anoint Jesus' body. They were met by a young man who told them that he had risen and they were to inform the disciples. They ran away in fear.

The Sabbath ended at sunset on Saturday. The shops then opened and the women would be able to make their purchases (verse 1). So it was early on Sunday morning that they went towards the tomb, to give the body the anointing which was due, according to Jewish custom. The women were the same as the three who had watched the crucifixion at a distance (xv. 40). Most people assume that the 'young man' who stood inside the tomb (verse 5) was an angel, but Mark uses the same Greek word as he does of the young man who ran away in Gethsemane at the arrest of Jesus (xiv. 51). Some think that it was the same youth; his white clothes might denote one of a higher social class. The special mention of Peter (verse 7) in the message to the disciples is an illustration of the special interest in him in this Gospel and may be evidence of his influence on the writer. The promise of an appearance in Galilee (verse 7—'as he told you' refers back to xiv. 28)

suggests that Mark had a tradition that it was there
that the disciples saw Jesus after the resurrection.

Mark's words about the reaction of the women are
very forceful—'fear and astonishment had gripped
them', apparently terror at the unexpected appearance
of the young man. Mark's language is also emphatic in
his statement that 'they said nothing to anybody' (verse
8). Perhaps he wished to emphasise that the belief in
the resurrection of Jesus was not dependent on the
women's story of an empty tomb, for they kept this to
themselves. The words 'for they were afraid' probably
supply the reason why they ran away, rather than the
reason why they said nothing about their fruitless visit
to the tomb. These words are the last ones of Mark's
Gospel as we have it. The oldest of the ancient witnesses
finish here. These include the most trustworthy manuscripts in Greek, such as the Vatican Codex (now in
Rome) and the Sinai Codex (now in the British Mu-
seum), and the oldest copies in the Latin, Syriac,
Armenian and other early translations. The ending is
very abrupt, for the sentence concludes with a Greek
conjunction (translated 'for'). The question whether
this was the way in which Mark ended his work has
been strenuously argued and is still unsettled.

It used to be thought that a Greek sentence could not
end in this way, but parallels have been adduced from
various types of Greek literature, including the Greek
translation of the Old Testament (Septuagint—LXX).
But it is not certain whether this could be the ending of a
complete book. Some have held that this is a suitable
ending to Mark's Gospel. The Gospel concludes on a
note of astonishment and awe, just as the account of the
beginning of Jesus' work had these features (i. 22–27).
The climax of the good news was reached; Jesus had

risen (xvi. 6); there was no need to tell of resurrection appearances foreshadowed in xvi. 7, for these were well known. But others think that Mark intended to conclude the book in a more fitting way, but for some reason he was unable and so it was left incomplete.

There is another possibility—that the original ending has been lost. Mark may have finished the sentence in some such way as 'they were afraid of what they had seen' or 'they were afraid of the Jews', and gone on to give an account of a meeting between Jesus and the disciples in Galilee. We do not know how this conclusion was lost; it might have been accidental. The last section of a long roll of papyrus would soon become worn with constant use or it might have been torn away in an attempt to rescue the book from the hands of some Roman during the persecution of the Christians. It was evidently felt in the early Church that the Gospel was incomplete, as more than one attempt was made to provide a suitable ending. The one which is found in most manuscripts is verses 9–20 in our Bibles.

A SUMMARY OF RESURRECTION APPEARANCES (verses 9–20)

This passage is omitted by the most trustworthy Greek manuscripts and the most important ancient versions. Church writers up to the fourth century state that the copies they used of Mark's Gospel did not contain it. Those manuscripts which do include it often have special marks to denote doubt on the part of the scribe.

In addition to this evidence, the style and vocabulary show that this is not really part of Mark's Gospel. Many unusual Greek words are found here and the style lacks the vividness and energy of Mark. The passage is evidently an attempt to finish the book in a suitable way. With verse 9 the account of the resurrection starts afresh, with no real connection with verse 8. Mary Magdalene is introduced as if for the first time, with a note as to who she was, although Mark has recently mentioned her (xvi. 1). The contents of the paragraph show that it was compiled from the other Gospels, especially Luke and John, which were of course written later than Mark. Thus the description of Mary comes from Luke viii. 2 (the statement that seven demons had been driven out of her is no reflection on her moral character. It probably means that she had been an epileptic or a neurotic). The appearance to her and her report to the disciples come from John xx. 18. The statement that they did not believe her (verse 11) reflects the reaction of the disciples in Luke xxiv. 11. The reference to the journey of two men into the country (verse 12) is a short summary of the story of the walk to Emmaus in Luke xxiv. 13ff. The account of the appearance to the eleven disciples at a meal (verse 14) reflects Luke xxiv. 41–43. The commission to the disciples to go and preach to the whole world (verse 15) is a summary of Luke xxiv. 47 and Matt. xxviii. 19. The statement that the disciples would exorcise and speak in 'new tongues' (verse 17) reflects the experiences of the early Church as recorded in the Acts; the reference to handling snakes (verse 18) is perhaps a reminiscence of Paul's experience at Malta (Acts xxviii. 3ff.), while the mention of drinking poisons without being hurt is in line with second-century legends about Christians who performed such marvellous feats. The description of the ascension (verse 19) is probably taken from Luke xxiv. 51.

ANOTHER SUMMARY

A further attempt to finish the Gospel is found in some manuscripts, either combined with verses 9–20 or by itself. The style and vocabulary show that this also is not Markan. It states that the women mentioned in verse 8 reported to Peter and his companions what they had been instructed and that Jesus sent out through them 'from east to west the sacred and imperishable proclamation of eternal salvation'.

INDEX OF SUBJECTS

Apocalypse, 154 ff.
Apostles, 72, 93, 96
Aramaic, 90

Baptism, 50 f.
Barabbas, 178
Beelzebub, 74
Bethany, 137, 164
Bethsaida, 99, 112
Blasphemy, 62, 75, 173
Boanerges, 72, 133

Caesarea Philippi, 112 ff.
Caiaphas, 171
Capernaum, 55, 124
Corban, 103
Covenant, 167 f.
Criticism, 3 ff.
Crucifixion, 178 f.

David's son, 25 f., 135
Decapolis, 88
Demon-possession, 56, 86 f.
Disciples, 72, 93

Elijah, 51, 112, 120
Essenes, 50
Exorcism, 56 f.

Family of Jesus, 74 f., 92
Form Criticism, 14 ff., 38 f.

Galilee, 34 f., 54

Gehenna, 127
Gethsemane, 169
Golgotha, 179
Gospel, 11 ff.

Herod Antipas, 94 ff.
Herodians, 71, 146
Herodias, 94 ff.

Inspiration, 1 ff.

Jairus, 88
James, 92
Jericho, 135
Jerusalem, 137 ff.
John, 125, 133
John the baptist, 49 ff., 94 ff., 143
John Mark, 29 ff.
Joseph of Arimathaea, 183
Judas Iscariot, 73, 165

Kingdom of God 54, 82 f., 117

Law (Jewish), 60, 66 ff., 101 ff.
Leprosy, 59
Levi, 64

Mark's Gospel:
  authorship, 29 ff.
  characteristics, 23 ff.
  conclusion, 186 ff.
  date, 32 ff.

historicity, 42 f.
'order', 24
place of writing, 33 f.
priority, 8 ff.
sources, 20 ff.
structure, 34 ff.
theology, 39 ff.
Mary of Magdala, 182, 188
Messiah, 25 ff., 49, 113, 115
Miracle stories, 16
Moses, 120

Nazareth, 91

Olives, mount of, 169
Oral period, 14 ff.

Papias, 21 f., 24
Parables, 77 ff., 144
Passover, 166 f.
Perea, 128
Peter, 21 f., 72, 169, 174 f., 185
Pharisees, 65, 101, 146
Phoenicia, 104
Pilate, 176 f.
Priests, 140, 143, 163
Pronouncement-stories, 15 f.

Q, 8
Qumran, 50

Resurrection, 114 f., 148, 185 ff.
Romans, 146 f., 177

Sabbath, 55, 67 ff., 70
Sadducees, 147 ff.
Sanhedrin, 143, 171, 176
Satan, 53, 74, 114
Scribes, 56, 150, 152
Servant of God, 53, 116, 121
Sinners, 65
Son of God, 49, 173, 182
Son of Man, 27 ff., 63, 115 ff., 121, 134, 160 f., 173
Source Criticism, 5 f.
Spirit of God, 52, 157
Synagogue, 55 f., 88
Synoptic problem, 6 ff.

Tax-collectors, 64 f.
Teaching of Jesus, 18 f., 29
Temple, 139 f., 156, 172, 182
Textual Criticism, 3 ff.
Traditions of the elders, 101 f.

Zealots, 73, 83